CONTENTS

T0070684

INTRODUCTION

Why another guitar instruction book?

I thought a long time about writing an instruction book for one simple reason: most of the available books on guitar are just too specific. The emphasis is too much on one topic: 10,000 guitar chords, sight-reading, harmony and theory, guitar techniques, guitar improvising, blues guitar, etc. They are probably good books, but they forget about the big picture. They never answer questions like: "How can I use what I learned in theory? *How* can I build chords that I can play on the guitar? *Why* should I learn sight-reading?"

I've chosen to combine the most important topics into one book, *How to Get Better at Guitar*, and hopefully answer the questions posed above. All the topics are connected with each other. You will see how to apply everything you learn. The book is divided into five chapters, each of which consists of four lessons. The first three lessons of each chapter are divided into the following sections: Harmony and Theory, Rhythm Concepts, Sight-Reading, and Scales and Techniques. Lesson four of each chapter will familiarize you with a different style. These will be arranged as such: blues, rock, Latin, funk, and jazz (one style per chapter).

This book shows you more than just the basics of guitar playing—it gives you a comprehensive education in music. If you are interested in becoming a good guitarist and a serious musician, you should enjoy this book immensely.

ABOUT THE AUTHOR

Thorsten Kober started to play the violin at the age of seven. He played in the high school orchestra and traveled to Britain, France, and Poland for several years. He picked up the guitar at the age of sixteen, after he thought that the guitar was the right instrument for him.

After playing in local bands in his home town for a while, he decided to study in Munich for two years at the Munich Guitar Institute.

Shortly afterwards he wanted to get serious and came to the States to study at G.I.T. (Musicians Institute) in Hollywood, where he graduated in 1997.

Since then he has been busy teaching, composing, recording, and performing, and has been seen playing guitar on commercials, TV shows, music videos, and movies.

Thorsten is endorsing Andreas Guitars, Seymour Duncan Pickups, Thomas-Infeld Strings, and Rocktron Products.

For more information, go to: *www.thorstenkober.com.*

HARMONY AND THEORY

Standard Notation

There are many different systems of notating music for the guitar. I will introduce these systems in their proper place, but I would like to begin with standard music notation. *Standard notation* may seem a little confusing at first; there is nothing to tell you where on the guitar to play a certain note. However, standard notation allows you to communicate with other musicians who have no familiarity with guitar-specific notational systems like tablature, chord diagrams, and scale diagrams.

In the Western tradition of music, notes are given letter names, sometimes altered with the words "sharp" (♯) or "flat" (♭). We use the letter names A through G. As notes move progressively higher in pitch, they move upwards through this seven-letter musical alphabet. When we reach the note G, we recycle the letter names to continue higher. Similarly, when we go down below A, we continue with G.

This extends as far as we can hear in both directions, but for practical purposes, we use a small portion of the total range at any one time to notate music. In order to show which note is which, we use a group of five lines (and the spaces in between them). This is called the *staff*:

The symbol at the left of the staff above is called a *treble clef*. There are several different clefs used in notating music, but two are by far the most commonly used: the treble clef and the bass clef. Since guitar music is written in the treble clef, we'll be dealing it with exclusively throughout this book. We'll take a look at the function of a clef in just a bit.

The five lines on the staff above, from low to high, represent the notes E, G, B, D, and F. The four spaces (in between the lines) from low to high represent the notes F, A, C, and E. The vertical placement of a note is in direct correlation to its relative sounding pitch. In other words, if a note is written lower on the staff, it will sound lower than one written higher on the staff. Notes themselves will always consist of a *head* (either solid or open), and often a *stem* and a *beam* or *flag*. If we need to extend notes above or below the staff, we use *ledger lines*, following the musical alphabet as we ascend or descend. The example below shows several notes on the staff (including some on ledger lines) and identifies the names of the notes:

The C note in the above example (first ledger line below the staff) is known as *middle C*. This note can be found in the middle of a piano's range and serves as a sort of "benchmark" when dealing with musical range. Because instruments have different ranges, the treble clef will not adequately suit every instrument. Take a bass guitar, for instance. If you were to try to notate a bass guitar piece on a treble clef staff, you would see nothing but ledger lines below the staff for most of the piece. This is where other clefs come in. The obvious alternative for a bass guitar piece would be the bass clef, seen below:

In the above staff, the bass clef essentially renames the lines and spaces to better suit the lower range of bass instruments. The lines from low to high represent the notes G, B, D, F, and A, while the spaces from low to high represent the notes A, C, E, and G. These notes are much lower in pitch than those represented by the treble clef. You can use middle C as a point of reference to illustrate this difference. In the bass clef, middle C is now located on the first ledger line *above* the staff. The example below demonstrates the same musical passage, as it would appear written in each clef:

As we can see, the treble clef is best suited for notes that fall above the range of middle C, while the bass clef is best suited for notes that fall below middle C.

Now that you have an idea about the function of clefs, let's get back to the treble clef. To build up your confidence in recognizing notes by name, try the exercise below. Remember that ledger lines progress through the musical alphabet just the same as the lines and spaces on the staff:

Write the name of each note underneath the staff:

Now let's add some rhythm to our notes. The way the head is written (solid or open) and the presence or absences of stems, beams, or flags all give us information about the rhythm of the note. We'll also come across *rests*. A rest tells us to be silent for a specified period of time. Recurring patterns of strong and weak beats create what is called *meter* and is indicated with a symbol that looks like a fraction at the beginning of a piece of music. The most common meter in music is 4/4 (four quarter) time. The top number tells us that there will be recurring groups of *four* notes, while the bottom number tells us that a *quarter* note will receive one beat. This fractional number is called a *time signature*. Below we'll find the most commonly used notes and rests and their durations:

Note Values

Whole note: four beats

Half note: two beats

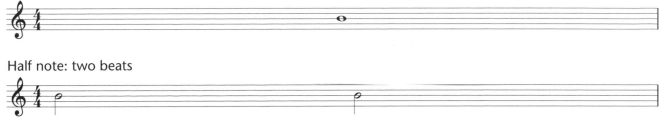

Quarter notes: one note per beat

Eighth notes: two notes per beat

Sixteenth notes: four notes per beat

Thirty-second notes: eight notes per beat

Rest Values

Whole rest

Half rests

Quarter rests

Eighth rests

Sixteenth rests

Thirty-second rests

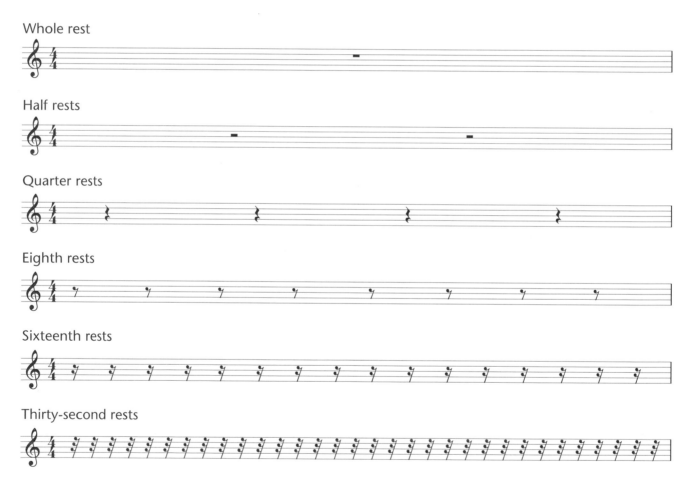

Tablature

The difference between *tablature* and standard notation is that with tablature you don't have to be able to read or name notes. Instead, you use numbers that represent exactly the fret and the string that is supposed to be played. The difficulty with reading notes is that there are several places on the fretboard to play the same note. That means that you have to decide where to play the note. Tablature makes this decision for you.

Instead of the five-line staff of standard notation, tablature uses six lines. Each line represents a string of the guitar.

The letters "TAB" in the beginning of the staff tell you that it is tablature. The top line represents the first string, which is the highest-sounding string. The bottom line represents the sixth string, which is the lowest-sounding string. The numbers placed on the lines represent the frets at which you play. The notes are read and played from left to right, just as in standard notation.

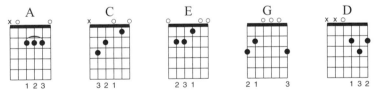

In the TAB staff above you would play:

the sixth string open, then at the third fret

the fifth string open, then at the second fret

the fourth string open, then at the second fret

the first and second strings at the third fret with the third string at the fourth fret simultaneously

the first string at the twelfth fret, then at the tenth fret

finally, the second string at the twelfth fret

The numbers represent the frets, not the fingering. In tablature, you don't see any time signatures or rhythmic notation. However, TAB staffs are usually presented in conjunction with standard notation, and therefore the rhythm and meter can be determined. If you come across some TAB without accompanying standard notation and without a recording to compare it to, you're pretty much in the dark as far as the rhythm goes.

Chord Diagrams

Above are some examples of *chord diagrams*. Chord diagrams are somewhat like tablature turned sideways: the six vertical lines represent the strings. The horizontal lines represent the frets, and the black dots represent where your fingers go. The numbers below each black-dotted string represent the fingers used. The X above a string tells you not to play that string, while the O tells you to play that string open (without any finger on it). The chord name appears above the diagram. So the first chord would be an A chord. (To be absolutely correct, it is an A major chord; major chords are so common that we often drop the "major" part of their names.) In it, the sixth string is crossed out (X), so you would not play that string; the fifth string is played open (O), the fourth, third, and second strings are played at the second fret with the first, second, and third fingers, and the first string is also played open (O).

Chord diagrams are commonly used as a shorthand method to avoid having to repeatedly write out full chords in TAB or standard notation.

Scale Diagrams

Scale diagrams are like a cross between chord diagrams and tablature. Like tablature, a scale diagram consists of six horizontal lines representing the strings. But unlike tablature, the notes are not read from left to right. Instead, the scale diagram represents all the possible choices of notes in a given scale. Like a chord diagram (turned sideways) the lines perpendicular to the strings are the frets. The Roman numeral tells you on which fret you start. In the example above it's the 5th fret. The circles represent the fingers of your left hand. It is common in scale diagrams for the "root" of the scale (or the note after which the scale is named) to be indicated in some fashion. This could include boxing or circling the note or coloring it differently. In the example above, the white circles indicate the root.

If you've forgotten Roman numerals (or never learned them!), here's a guide:

I	II	III	IV	V	VI	VII	VIII	IX	X
1	2	3	4	5	6	7	8	9	10

XI	XII	XIII	XIV	XV	XVI	XVII	XVIII	XIX	XX
11	12	13	14	15	16	17	18	19	20

RHYTHM CONCEPTS

Using the Metronome

Everything you practice on the guitar should be practiced "in time." That means you should always use something that keeps the time for you. A metronome, a drum machine, a rhythmic CD jam track—these are all good ways to practice in time. But the metronome is perhaps the best because it is so simple and can be adjusted to so many speeds. There are several ways that you can use a metronome:

1. The metronome is usually set to give you quarter notes, or one click per beat. The number on the metronome gives you the number of beats per minute (60 = 60 bpm). If you play a song in 4/4, you count like this: "ONE-two-three-four, ONE-two-three-four," etc.; one count per click. If you are in 3/4, you count like this: "ONE-two-three, ONE-two-three," etc. Remember that the bottom number of the time signature tells you the kind of note that gets one beat (in these cases, a quarter note), while the top number tells you how many beats (or counts) are in one measure.

2. If you have a song in "cut time" (2/2), you count like this: "ONE-two, ONE-two," etc. Here you only have two beats per measure.

3. You can also use the metronome on the "backbeats." This is very difficult, but many jazz musicians use it to build their sense of "swing." Here the metronome clicks on the "two" and "four" of the measure.

Let's put our rhythmic notation to work now. Again, start all the exercises slowly! Even if the rhythms look easy, they can be tricky when you sight-read them. Always look for the smallest note value to determine at what tempo you want to start and ALWAYS use a metronome. Tap your foot to the metronome and be sure it's synchronized before you start to play. Use any one note to play through the exercises first, getting a feel for the rhythm. I use the fourth fret on the third string. Make sure you let the note ring as long as you are supposed to. Mute the string at the rests; believe it or not, this is a very common mistake for a lot of people. If you make a mistake, stop, isolate the rhythm figure, and repeat the figure until you feel comfortable with it. Repeat the line that contains the figure again and move on. As I said, keep it slow, because you want to get to the point where you can read "ahead" at least one or two measures to keep the music flowing. If you're having trouble keeping up with the metronome, your tempo is too fast.

Rhythm Exercise 1

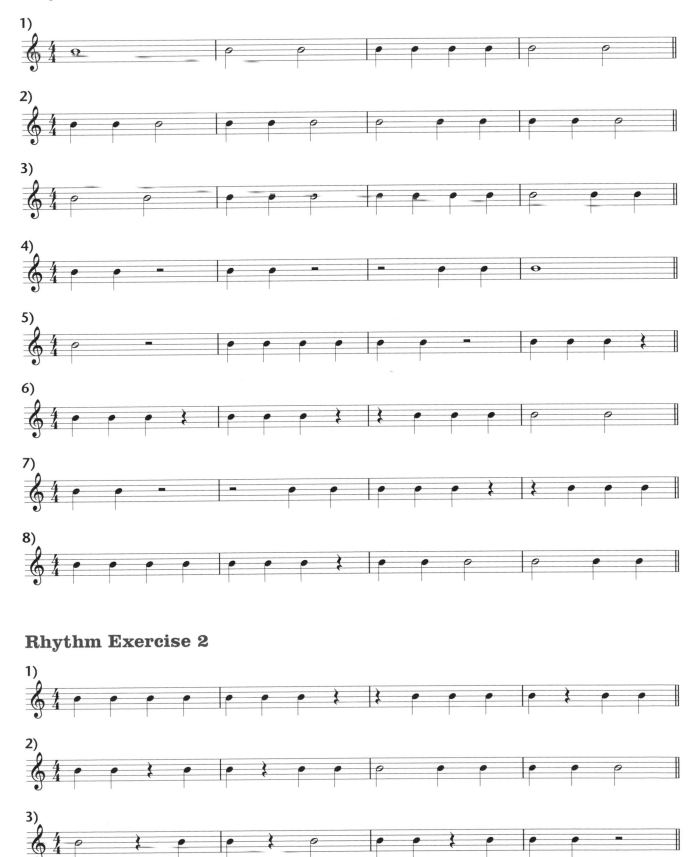

Rhythm Exercise 2

Open String Chords

Open string chords are chords that are played using open strings. All the chords in this lesson are in root position, which means that the lowest note of the chord is the note that gives the chord its name. There are many variations for these chords; we'll start with the basic ones.

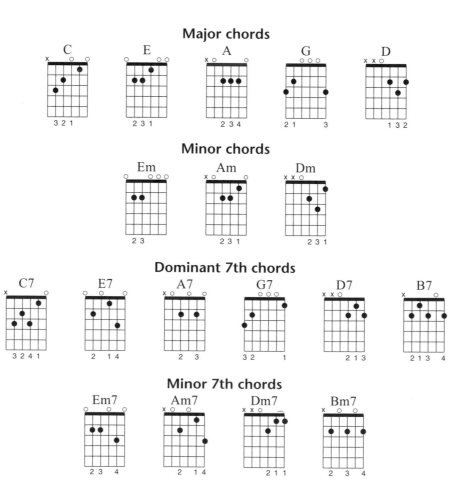

Major 7th chords

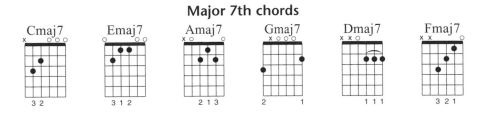

As an additional exercise, try playing the rhythms in Rhythm Exercises 1 and 2 using some of these chords.

SIGHT-READING

Sight-reading is one of those skills that many guitarists don't even bother learning. It seems so much more convenient to just learn how to read tablature or pick up bits and pieces from friends and fellow musicians. This is all well and good, but I like to think of sight-reading as another tool that we have available that can be of great benefit. It enables you to read any music written for any instrument and it allows you to choose where you want to play a certain note instead of locking yourself into a certain position. Of course, it takes some effort to memorize the notes and their places on the guitar, but the reward is worthwhile; it can be a great joy to be able to read music fluently. The key to successful sight-reading is to keep it slow, tackle just a little at a time, use a metronome to pace yourself, and be patient. As you begin to develop your sight-reading skills, use everything you can find, even if it is not especially for guitar. Don't memorize the songs or examples, as this will defeat the purpose. Alternate the songs in your daily practice routine, as this will delay the memorization process.

We'll first learn the open strings on the guitar. I call them your reference notes. You can use them to help find the notes in between in the beginning. At first I'll give you the standard notation and the tablature for reference, but soon the tablature will be gone, so memorize those note locations!

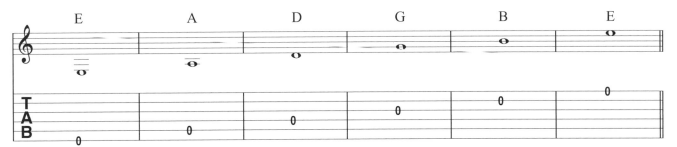

C Major Scale: First or Open Position

Here we see the C major scale on the guitar. Major scales are the foundation of our musical system; you'll recognize their sound instantly. C major is a good one to begin with because it uses no sharps or flats. This is in first or open position—"first" because the first finger is in the first fret, and "open" because whenever we can, we use open strings. The numbers to the left of the notes in the standard notation indicate which fingers of the left hand to use: 1 = index finger, 2 = middle finger, 3 = ring finger, and 4 = pinky.

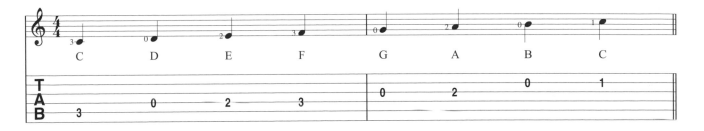

How about the other notes from the C major scale in first position? Here they are:

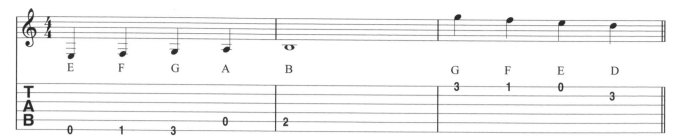

E   F   G   A   B   G   F   E   D

To tie it all together, here's a C major scale in first position with upper and lower extensions.

Remember to practice this slowly, tackle just a little at a time, and use the metronome to pace yourself.

For practice, write the name of each note underneath the staff:

1)

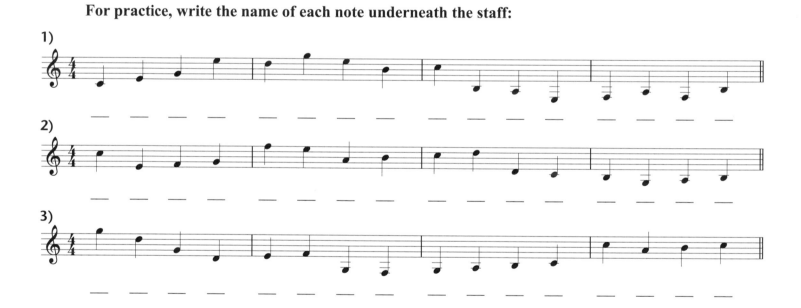

2)

3)

Now let's tackle some real sight-reading using what we've learned so far.

Sight-Reading Exercise 1

C major, first position

Sight-Reading Exercise 2

C major, first position

SCALES AND TECHNIQUES

Warm-up Exercise

This first exercise is one of the few that really helps. Don't practice this for speed! It is more important that you try to get a good, smooth sound from each note that you play. Let each note sound as long as possible. Don't mute any note and don't play any note *staccato* (short). Remember to use the metronome and start at a slow tempo! Be careful how you use your left hand on this exercise. Don't lift your fingers too far from the strings. Keep them above the strings, as if they were about to play, even if you don't need them. Play the exercise with alternate (down-up) picking, as indicated by the arrows below the notes. Once you get the feel of the exercise, try not to watch your hands.

🔊 Track 1

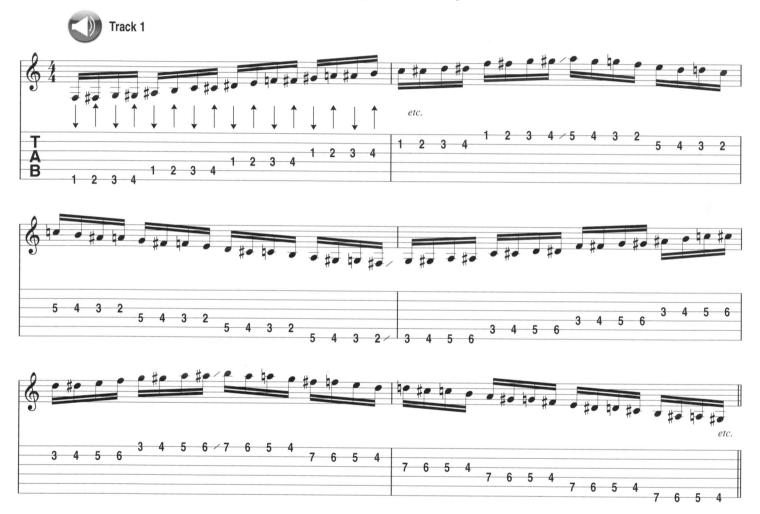

As a variation, start this exercise on the seventh fret and work your way down, shifting the fourth finger down one fret each time instead of up. Give each finger one fret and make sure that you use your fingertips. Don't lay your fingers flat on the strings. Practice this exercise VERY slowly—it's not a speed exercise.

Pentatonic Scales

In contrast to the seven-note major scale we learned earlier, *pentatonic scales* consist of five different notes. Here we're going to learn the A minor pentatonic scale in its five forms over the entire guitar neck.

The numbers below the scale indicate the scale degree. We number scale degrees by how the notes relate to the notes of a major scale. In a major scale for instance, the degrees would simply be: 1–2–3–4–5–6–7; in A major, these notes would be: A–B–C♯–D–E–F♯–G♯ (we know this because the key signature of A major has three sharps). In a minor scale, we lower the 3rd, 6th, and 7th scale degrees by a half step. So an A minor scale looks like this: 1–2–♭3–4–5–♭6–♭7. The "♭3," "♭6," and "♭7" tell us that we should lower C♯, F♯, and G♯ by a half step, so we end up with: A–B–C–D–E–F–G.

In a minor pentatonic scale, we're only using five of the seven notes of a minor scale: the 1st (root), ♭3rd, 4th, 5th, and ♭7th, or A–C–D–E–G.

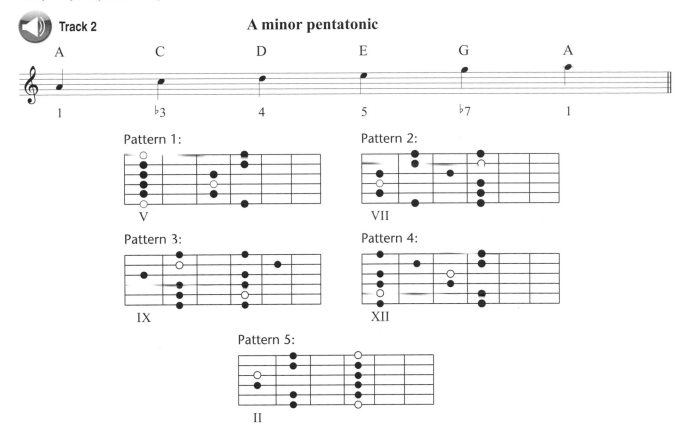

The A minor pentatonic scale also goes by another name: C major pentatonic. The notes are the exact same in each scale, but there is one difference. In A minor pentatonic, we're thinking of the A note as the root of the scale; in C major pentatonic, we're thinking of C as the root. So the degrees of the scale are renamed as such. Note that the patterns of the scale are renamed as well. Pattern 1 here has C as the root, whereas pattern 1 of A minor pentatonic had A as the root.

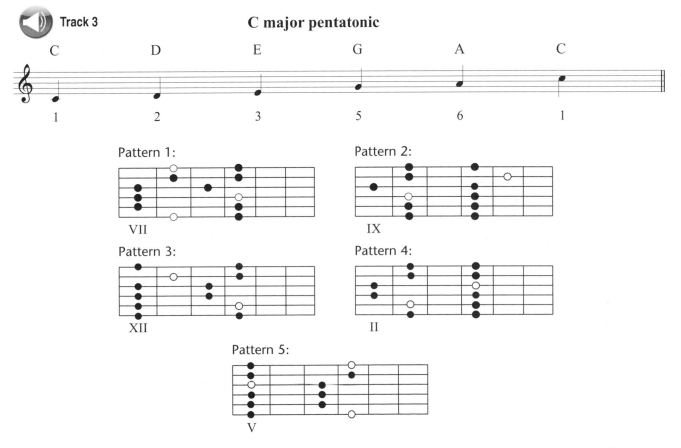

LESSON 2

HARMONY AND THEORY

Major Scale Construction

In Lesson 1, we learned how to play the C major scale in first position. Let's take a closer look at the notes in that scale to see how it's constructed. In order to understand this construction, we need to understand the concept of *half steps* and *whole steps*. A half step is fairly easy to understand on the guitar; it is simply the distance of one fret. For example, the distance from the third fret, fifth string to the fourth fret, fifth string is a half step. A whole step is the distance of two frets on the guitar—from the third fret, fifth string to the fifth fret, fifth string, for example. Playing through the C major scale, you should notice something interesting: There are more places where the notes progress in whole steps than where they progress in half steps. If we were to number the degrees of the C major scale, we would see that between the 3rd (E) and 4th (F) degrees and 7th (B) and 1st (C) degrees we have half steps. Between all the other degrees of the scale we have whole steps. This "formula" of whole steps and half steps is the building block for the major scale. It looks like this: whole–whole–half–whole–whole–whole–half. The example below demonstrates this as it applies to our C major scale. I've written the scale out on one string in the TAB so you can clearly see the two fret/whole step and one fret/half step relationship:

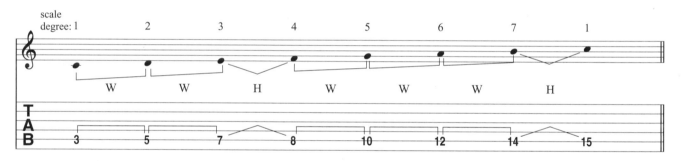

You'll notice in the above example that when we move from B (7) to C, we start numbering again at 1. This C is said to be one *octave* higher than the C we started on. This is why we start over with the numbers; the notes are all the same—they're just an octave higher.

This formula will remain the same for any major scale in any key, as we'll see later on.

Bar Lines

With the help of the *bar line,* you divide a piece of music into smaller parts, making it easier to follow. If bar lines weren't used, music would look very disorganized and become very hard to keep track of:

We use the bar line to indicate where each bar (or measure) begins and ends. This coincides with the time signature and allows us to keep track of the music more easily:

How long is a bar? This depends on the time signature. As we discussed before, the time signature consists of two numbers. The top number tells us how many beats will be in each bar (or measure), and the bottom number tells us which rhythmic note value will be considered one beat. The most common time signatures are 4/4 and 3/4. This means that you have either four quarter notes (4/4) or three quarter notes (3/4) in one bar.

You may have noticed the two lines at the end of the above example. This is called a *double bar line.* These are used to indicate the end of a larger section of the music (such as the verse, chorus, bridge, etc.).

Repeats

We use *repeat signs* as a way to avoid writing out the same music twice. They mark a part of a song that should be repeated exactly. They look like this:

In the above example, once you reach the repeat sign at the right, you would begin again at the left. After you have repeated the phrase, you would continue past the repeat sign to the rest of the song. Occasionally you will see additional instructions at the end of the section, such as: "play 3 times," or "3x." This would indicate that the music within the repeat signs should be played three times before you move on to the rest of the song.

Accidentals

Thus far, we've dealt only with notes in the C major scale: C–D–E–F–G–A–B. However, between some of these notes, there are "in between" notes; this is where *accidentals* come in. A *sharp* symbol (♯) placed in front of a note raises that note by one half step, while a *flat* symbol (♭) placed in front lowers that note by one half step. Let's look again at our C major scale that we played entirely on the fifth string. If we were to play all twelve notes between C at the third fret and the C an octave higher at the fifteenth fret, we would need to use accidentals for some of the notes. These twelve consecutive half steps would be known as the *chromatic scale.* Since it includes all twelve notes, the chromatic scale doesn't really have a "root." It's simply named by which note it begins and ends on. Below we see the ascending chromatic scale in C:

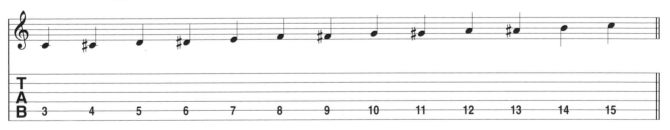

As a very general rule, sharps are usually used when ascending in pitch (as seen above), while flats are usually used when descending in pitch:

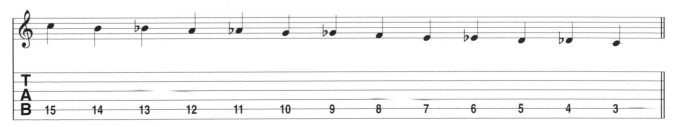

You may have noticed in the above examples that one note can have two different names. For example, in the ascending chromatic scale, the fourth fret was called C♯. In the descending chromatic scale, however, this note was called D♭. These notes are said to be *enharmonic*. It simply means that they are the same note; they're just named differently sometimes because of their function.

Occasionally, you will see double sharp symbols (𝄪) and double flat symbols (♭♭). These raise or lower the pitch of the note by two half steps (or one whole step).

Key Signatures

The *key signature* is another time-saving device used in music notation. It is always found at the beginning of the staff directly after the clef. Here are some examples of key signatures:

Key signatures can contain either flats or sharps. The accidentals written in the staff tell you that they should be played throughout the whole song. For example, in the top staff above, you would play F♯ instead of F and C♯ instead of C throughout the whole piece.

Here are the key signatures for all the keys:

C Major: no sharps or flats	F Major: B♭
G Major: F♯	B♭ Major: B♭, E♭
D Major: F♯, C♯	E♭ Major: B♭, E♭, A♭
A Major: F♯, C♯, G♯	A♭ Major: B♭, E♭, A♭, D♭
E Major: F♯, C♯, G♯, D♯	D♭ Major: B♭, E♭, A♭, D♭, G♭
B Major: F♯, C♯, G♯, D♯, A♯	G♭ Major: B♭, E♭, A♭, D♭, G♭ C♭
F♯ Major: F♯, C♯, G♯, D♯, A♯, E♯	

(Note that F♯ major and G♭ major are enharmonic. These two keys will sound exactly the same, but since they have six accidentals in either sharps or flats, you will see this key written in both.)

There is one more symbol that you will see next to a note that alters its pitch. This is called the *natural* sign (♮). This symbol has two functions.

The first function deals with the key signature. As we said before, a key signature indicates that you are to play a sharp or flat every time to see a note throughout the entire song. There are times, however, when you don't want a note to be raised or lowered. For these occasions, the natural sign is used to temporarily cancel out the sharp or flat of the key signature. That note will then be played as a natural (not sharp or flat) through the duration of that measure. After that, it will return to its raised or lowered state as indicate by the key signature. In the example below, you would play these notes: D–C♯–D–C.

The second function of the natural symbol is to correct an accidental that is not part of the key signature. For example, if you're in the key of C major, which has no sharps or flats in its key signature, and you come across an F♯ in the music, you would use a natural symbol on the F when you'd like it to return to normal. The sharp will affect the F for the duration of the measure; after that it would return to its normal state as indicated in the key signature. If you need it to return before that though, you need to use the natural sign. In the example below, you would play these notes: E–F–F♯–G–A–G–F.

RHYTHM CONCEPTS

Triplets

Triplets indicate that you are to play three notes in the space that you would normally play two. See below:

Half notes: play three half notes in the time of 2.

Quarter notes: play three quarter notes in the time of 2.

Eighth notes: play three eighth notes in the time of 2.

Sixteenth notes: play six sixteenth notes in the time of 4.

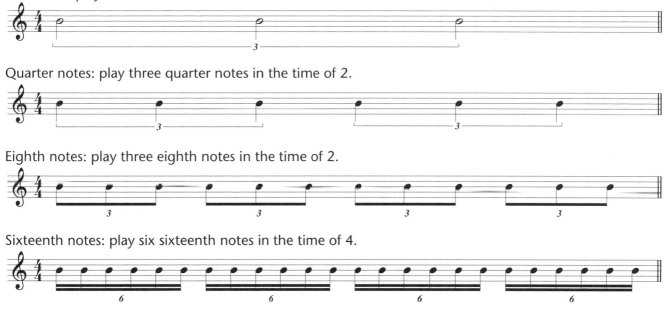

Here's how triplets look when applied to rests:

Half rests:

Quarter rests:

Eighth rests:

Sixteenth rests:

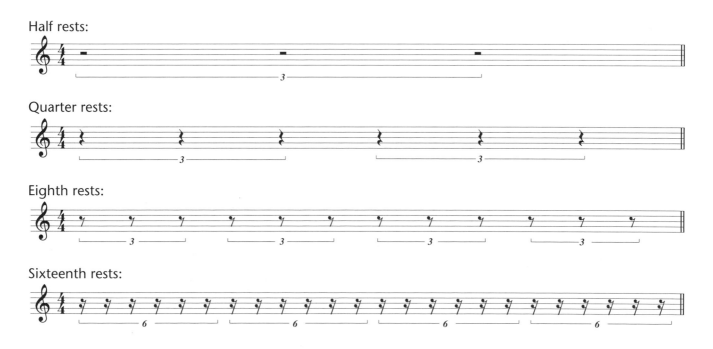

As you can see, any beat, group of beats, or division of a beat that is normally divided in two can also be divided in three with the use of triplets. What's more, they can be divided into other groupings as well: 5, 7, etc. The number within the bracket tells you how many notes you should play instead the normal amount. Triplets, however, are by far the most common division you will encounter.

Rhythm Exercise 3

Rhythm Exercise 4

Barre Chords

Barre chords are named as such because they require one or more fingers to "barre" (or lay flat) across several strings at once. The first finger is usually the one doing the barring. This will require some serious finger strength if you're not used to this and will probably take a little while to master. Don't be disappointed if you can't play these right away; most people can't when they first try. Stick with it though; these chord forms are invaluable for when you need to play in keys that don't allow many open-string chords. Since barre chords are often not played in open or first position, a fret indicator tells you where the shape is to be played on the neck. In these examples, the "5fr" marking indicates that these chords are to be played with your first finger barring across the fifth fret. Here we see some major, minor, and 7th barre chord forms built on both the sixth and fifth strings. The great thing about these chord forms is that they are moveable. This means that by shifting, for example, the first A chord form up two frets, you are playing a B major chord. By shifting it down one fret, you're playing an A♭ (or G♯) major chord.

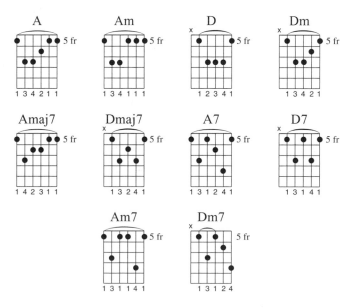

You can use the open string chord forms that we learned in Lesson 1 to form barre chord shapes as well. Take an open-string form C major chord, for example. If you re-fret this chord with fingers 2, 3, and 4 instead of 1, 2, and 3 and then imagine that your first finger is "barring" the open strings as a fret, you can see the moveable form. This moveable form is often named after the open-string chord form from which it originated. You can see several examples of this below:

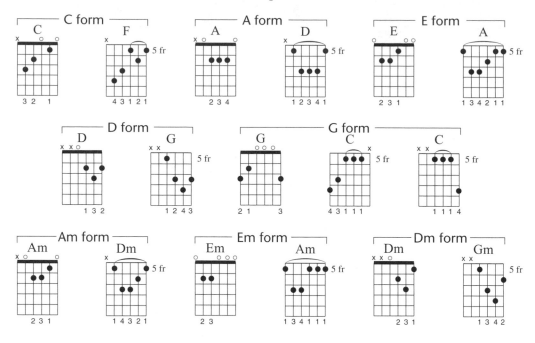

SIGHT-READING

Positions

The term *position* is used to identify where on the guitar neck we are playing. If we are playing a scale shape in which our first finger occupies the fifth fret, we say that we are in "fifth position." The position is always determined by the location of the first finger—even if we're not using the first finger. For example, if we were playing the notes B and C on the sixth string (frets 7 and 8) with our third and fourth fingers, we would still call this fifth position, because our first finger would end up on fret 5 if we laid our fingers on the fretboard in a one-finger-per-fret fashion.

Below we see eight different positions of the C major scale. In each position, we start with the lowest possible note that belongs to the C major scale and play up through to the highest.

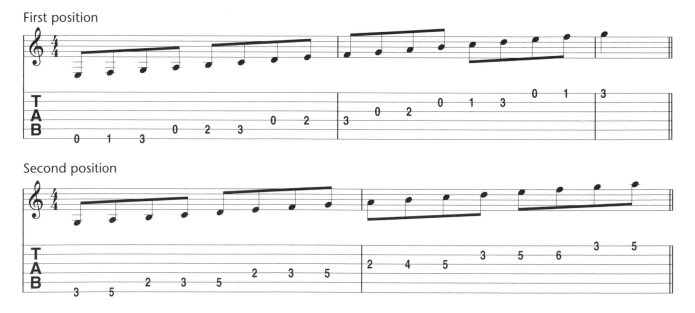

Fifth position

Seventh position

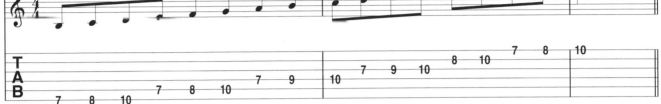

Tenth position

Twelfth position

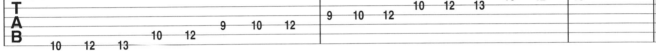

Sight-Reading Exercise 3

C major, first position

Sight-Reading Exercise 4

C major, first position

SCALES AND TECHNIQUES

Pentatonic Scale Sequences

We use the term *sequence* when we repeat the melodic contour of a phrase beginning at a different note. For example, a sequence from a C major scale might be these notes played as triplets: C–D–E, D–E–F, E–F–G, F–G–A, etc. As you can see, we're *sequencing* this three-note scale motive through the scale, each time beginning one note higher. Sequences are certainly not limited to a structure this rigid; the word "sequence" is generally used to describe any type of repeating motive from which a pattern can be determined.

We're going to apply some different sequences now to pattern 1 of the A minor pentatonic scale we learned in Lesson 1. The numbers in parentheses represent the scale degrees of the pentatonic scale and tell us the order of each sequence.

🔊 **Track 4**

1) Groups of 3 (1-2-3, 2-3-4, 3-4-5, 4-5-1, etc.)

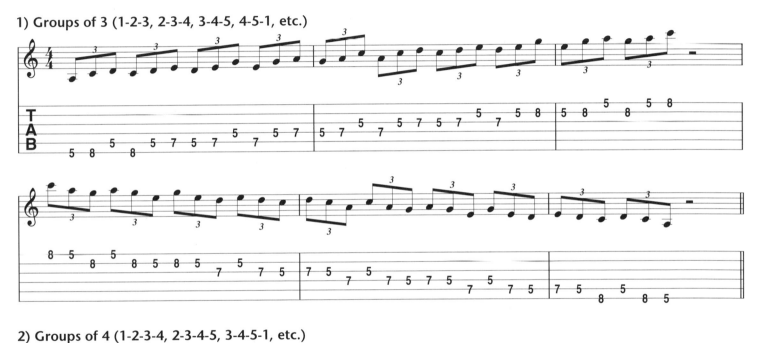

2) Groups of 4 (1-2-3-4, 2-3-4-5, 3-4-5-1, etc.)

3) (1-3-2-4-3-5-4-1, etc.)

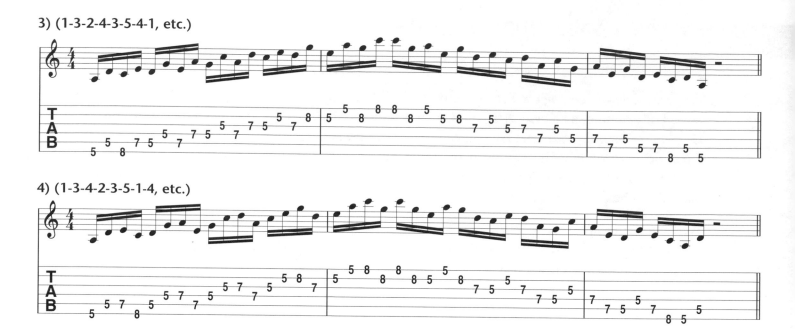

4) (1-3-4-2-3-5-1-4, etc.)

Extended Pentatonic Scales

In Lesson 1, you learned the fingering for the A minor pentatonic scale in its five patterns spanning the whole guitar neck. This will allow you to play phrases in many different places on the guitar, but many players will connect these positions together with what we call *extended pentatonic scales*. In the examples below, we'll begin in one scale pattern and move up the neck to others by sliding either our third or fourth finger along the string. In these examples, some strings will contain two notes, and others (that feature a slide) will contain three. As a variation, try playing these phrases backwards by using your first finger to slide down the string. See if you can find your own ways to connect the different patterns of the pentatonic scale together.

🔊 **Track 5**

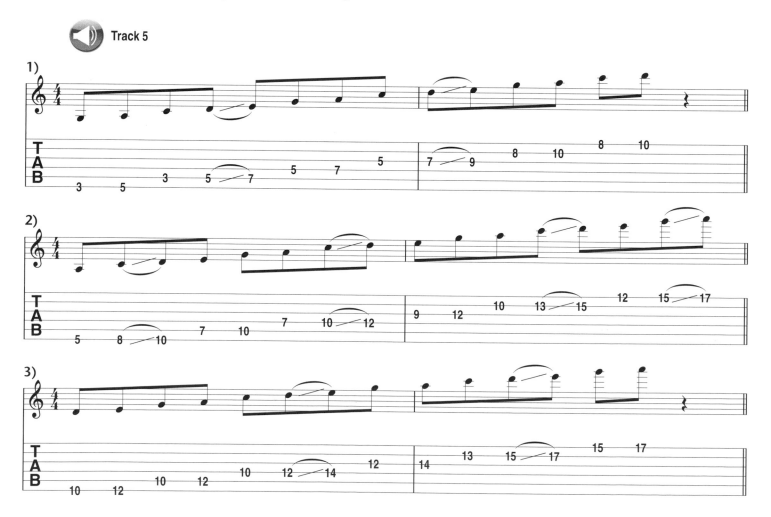

LESSON 3

HARMONY AND THEORY

Beams

The lines you've seen connecting some notes at the end of their stems are called *beams*. They are used, much like bar lines, to make the task of reading music easier. Whole notes, half notes, and quarter notes don't receive beams; only eighth notes and those shorter in duration do. As you can see from the example below, eighth notes use one beam, sixteenths use two beams, and thirty-second notes (very fast notes) use three beams. The number of beams directly coincides with the duration of the notes.

Flags

When eighth or sixteenth notes are by themselves and not linked by beams, they have *flags* attached to them. The number of flags for each note is the same as the number of beams: 1 for eighth notes, 2 for sixteenth notes, etc. See below for an example:

Ties

When you see two notes connected by a *tie,* it means you are to sustain the first note through the duration of the tied note. In the example below, the half note is tied to a quarter note, indicating that you hold it for three quarter notes (one half note plus one quarter note). The quarter note with the eighth note tied to it now has the length of three eighth notes (one quarter note plus one eighth note). The quarter note that is tied to another quarter note would now be the length of a half note.

Dots

A *dot* after a note increases the length of that note by 50 percent of its original length. See below for and example of dotted notes.

This means:

> a dotted whole note is held for the duration of six quarter notes
>
> a dotted half note is held for the duration of three quarter notes
>
> a dotted quarter note is held for the duration of three eighth notes
>
> a dotted eighth note is held for the duration of three sixteenth notes
>
> a dotted sixteenth note is held for the duration of three thirty-second notes

Chord Charts

Many times, *chord charts* are used as an efficient method to identify the chords and/or the form of a song. The chord symbols are written above the staff, and slashes (or hashmarks) indicate for how many beats you are to play each chord. In the example below, you would play each chord for one full measure (four beats).

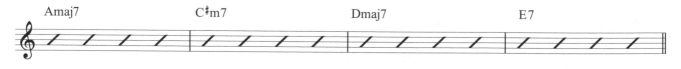

In the example below, we are introduced to the concept of *first* and *second endings*. This is another device used to avoid writing out the same material twice. In this example, you would play through the first four measures and then repeat from the beginning. The second time, however, after playing the first two measures, you would skip to the second ending and continue from there. So the complete first eight measures would be this: Em7–Am–Em7–Am7–Em7–Am–Am7–B7. The symbols in the last staff (:||) indicate that you are to repeat the chord pattern from the measure before.

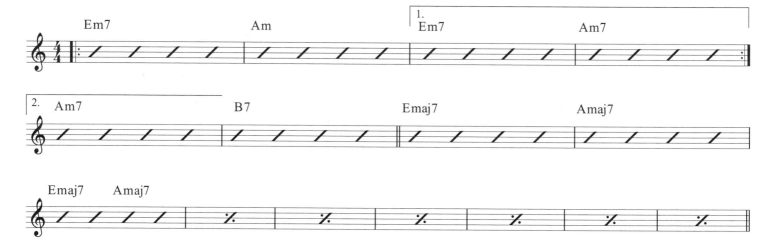

RHYTHM CONCEPTS

In Rhythm Exercises 5 and 6, we see the inclusion of ties and dotted notes for the first time.

Rhythm Exercise 5

Rhythm Exercise 6

Power Chords

Power chords are two-note chords consisting of the 1st and 5th degrees of a major scale. In the examples below, the notes would be A and E. The chords in row 1b feature another root (1st) note to give the chord a slightly bigger sound. The chords in rows 2a and 2b are known as *inversions*. This means that a note other than the root (A) is in the bass; in this case, it's the 5th (E). Finally, the last row of power chords are in dropped D tuning. In *dropped D tuning,* you tune your low E string down a whole step to D.

1a) Two-note voicings:

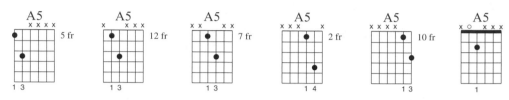

1b) Three-note voicings:

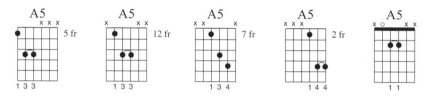

2a) Inversions:

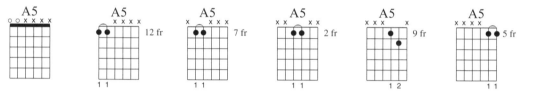

2b)

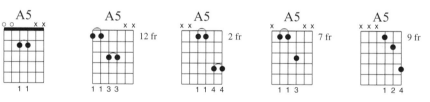

3) Dropped D Tuning:

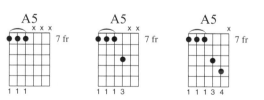

SIGHT-READING

Sight-reading Exercises 5 and 6 are designed to further familiarize you will the C major scale in first position.

Sight-Reading Exercise 5

C major, first position

Sight-Reading Exercise 6

C major, first position

SCALES AND TECHNIQUES

Blues Scales

By adding one note to our minor pentatonic scale, we create what is known as the *blues scale.* The note we add is the $\flat 5$ degree; in A minor pentatonic, this would be E$\flat$. Below we see the patterns of the A minor blues scale.

 Track 6

A minor blues scale

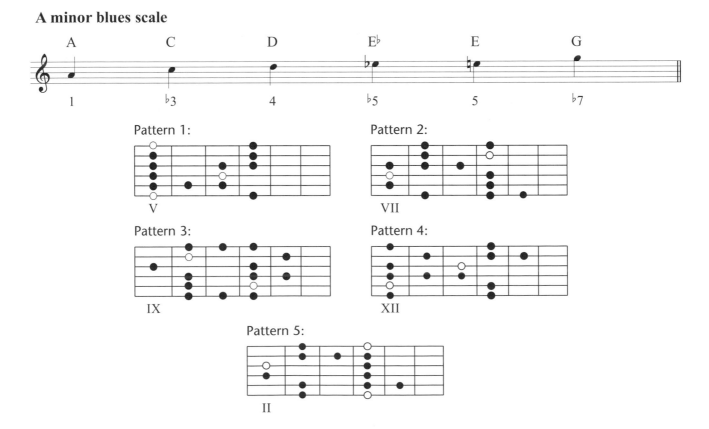

We can add this blue note to our C major pentatonic as well. Below we see the patterns of the C major blues scale. Remember, these are the same notes as the A minor blues scale; they're just renumbered to function differently in C major.

C major blues scale

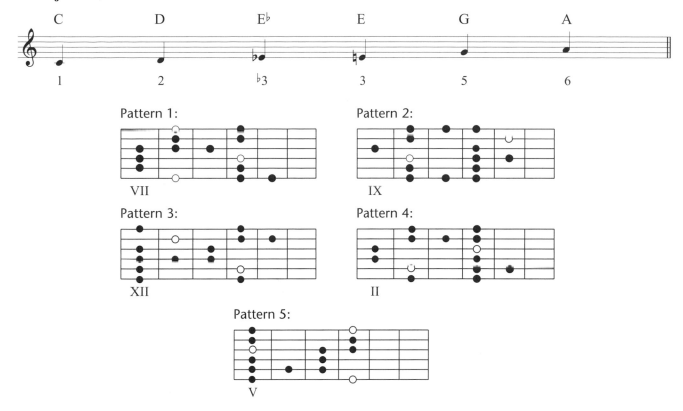

Repeating Patterns

Now we're going to learn some *repeating patterns* using the A minor pentatonic scale that you can use when soloing. Examples 1a, 1b, 2a, and 2b provide the basic patterns. Examples 3 and 4 move the 2a pattern through horizontal and vertical treatments, while examples 5 and 6 do the same with the 1b pattern.

 Track 8

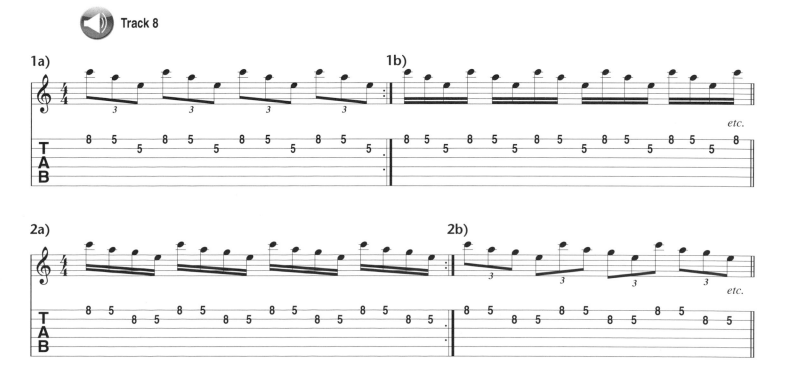

3) Horizontal movement

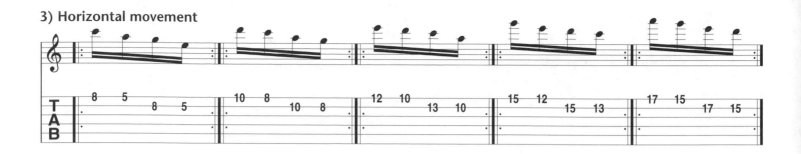

4) Vertical movement

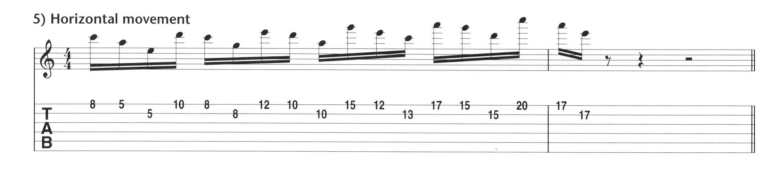

5) Horizontal movement

6) Vertical movement

Bends and Slides

Now we're going to treat our A minor pentatonic and blues scales to two expressive techniques: *bends* and *slides*. In the examples below, we're going to be bending the D note on the seventh fret, third string up a whole step to the note E. Using your third finger on the note with the first and second fingers behind it for support, bend the string up until the pitch matches the note E. You can test this by bending the note and then checking the pitch against the E on the second string, fifth fret. For the remaining E and A notes on the fifth frets, use your first finger and "roll" the pressure from the second string to the first string. You could also barre the first two strings and let the notes ring together; these licks are commonly played using both methods.

In the next example, we see a variation of our bending lick, as well as a sliding lick that makes use of the A minor blues scale. For the slide, use the third finger to slide up the E♭ and back down to the D again.

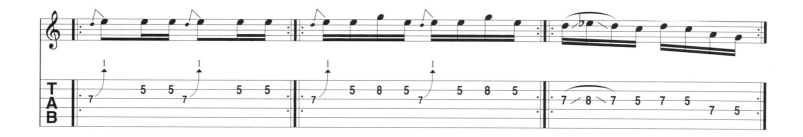

LESSON 4 • BLUES

BLUES CHORD PROGRESSIONS

12-Bar Blues

The *12-bar blues* is one of the most commonly used progressions in music. Here we're going to learn its form and many variations. Below we find a basic 12-bar blues in A. The three chords used are A7, D7, and E7. These three chords are built from the 1st, 4th, and 5th degrees of an A major scale. We therefore call them the I, IV, and V chords in the key of A.

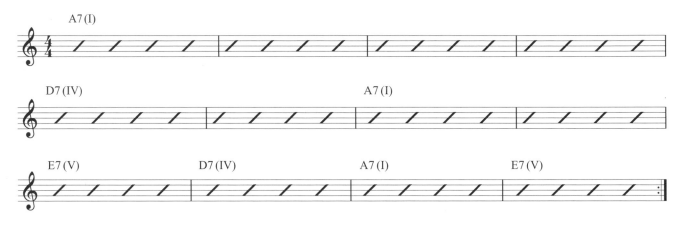

A very common variation on the standard 12-bar (perhaps even more common than the standard progression) is called the "quick-change." The only difference here is that in measure 2 we move to the IV chord (D7). In measure 3 we move back to the I chord and finish the rest of the progression the same way as we did before. Here's a quick-change blues in A:

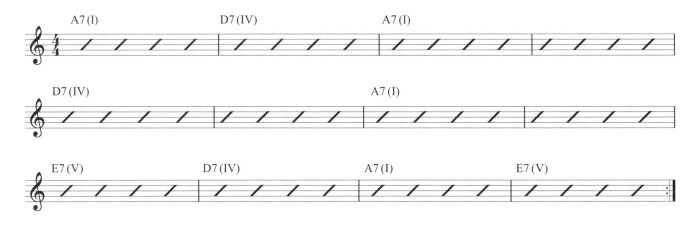

12-Bar Minor Blues

In a *minor blues*, the main difference is that we replace all the 7th chords with minor 7th chords. There is one other difference that appears in measures 9 and 10. We see a ♭IV chord (F7) moving to the V chord (E7). Notice also that the minor chords are labeled with lower case Roman numerals. This is commonly used as an efficient method to avoid having to write major or minor after a Roman numeral. If, for example, you saw a i–IV–V progression in A, you would know to play Am–D–E.

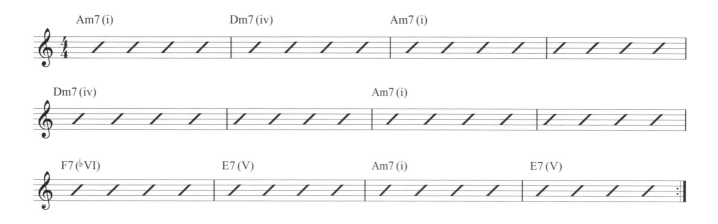

Here we see a variation on the minor blues. The only difference is in measures 9 and 10. If you're unfamiliar with some of these chords, I suggest getting your hands on a chord dictionary or chord book. There are many books like this available that teach you several ways to play most of the chords you'll ever come across.

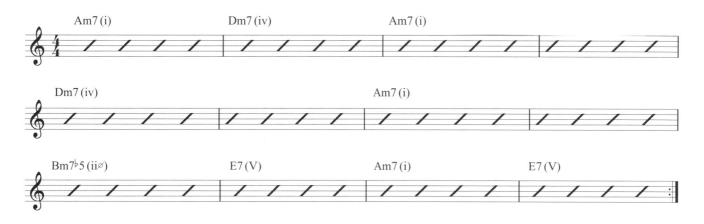

12-Bar Jazz Blues

In a *jazz blues,* we'll find a more harmonically complex approach to the 12-bar. There are many more chords present that produce tension and resolution throughout. In measures 7–10, we see the classic I–VI–ii–V progression—a staple in jazz standard repertoire. This progression is repeated again in measures 11 and 12, with each chord occupying only two beats instead of four.

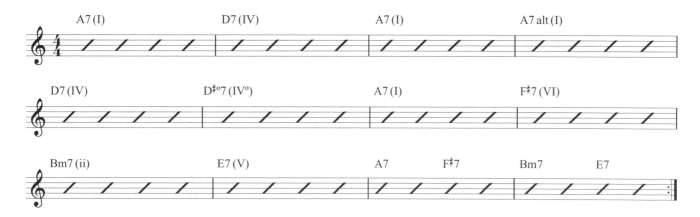

8-Bar Blues

Here we see an *8-bar blues* in its standard form.

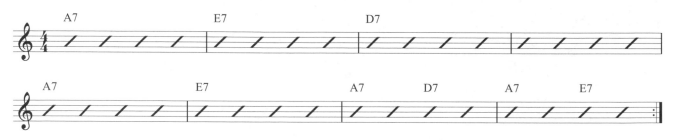

8-Bar Blues Variation

And now we see a variation on the 8-bar blues:

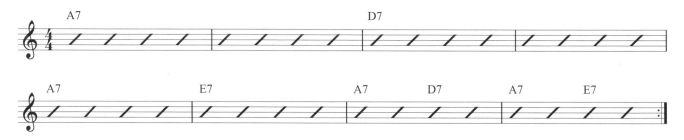

8-Bar Jazz Blues

Here we see a variation on the jazz blues that contains only eight measures.

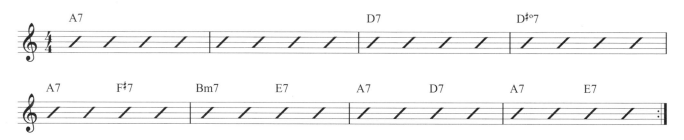

16-Bar Blues

The *16-bar blues* demonstrates a less common variation to the standard 12-bar. The E7 chord in parentheses at the end indicates that this chord is sometimes played and sometimes not.

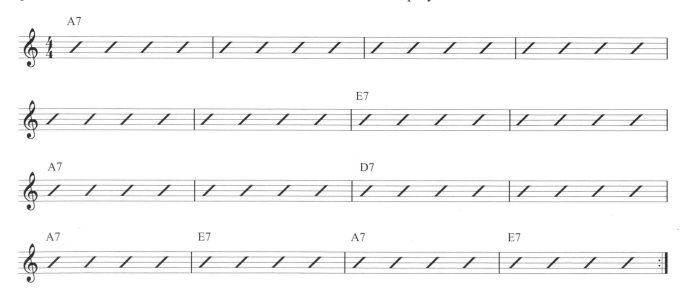

Intros, Endings, and Turnarounds

Several times blues tunes feature an introduction or ending that differs from the standard form. We'll take a look at some of these as well as some different turnarounds that you may come across from time to time.

Intro: From the Turnaround

This intro would be the same as starting from measure 9 in a 12-bar blues.

Intro: From the V Chord

Here's another four-measure intro that you will commonly see.

Outro: Break on the IV Chord

In an *outro*, the band will many times stop for a measure for dramatic effect. This space is usually filled by a concluding vocal line or guitar lick that indicates the tune has come to an end. Notice the rest markings in measure 2 after the first beat. This tells you to play the D7 chord on beat 1 and then rest for the remainder of the measure.

Outro: Break on the I Chord

Here we see the break one measure later.

Turnarounds

The *turnaround* occurs in measures 9–12 of a 12-bar blues. Its function is to wrap things up in the progression and set up momentum for another twelve bars. Below we'll find four common variations of the turnaround.

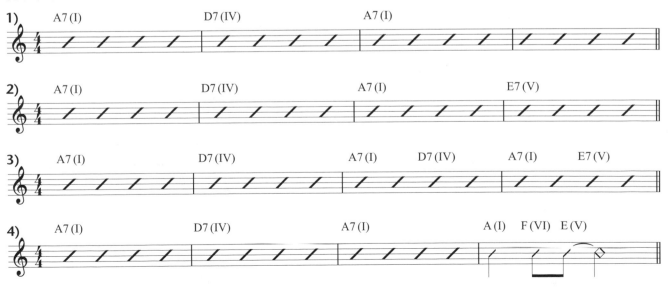

RHYTHM FIGURES

Two-Note Patterns

This is perhaps the most common type of rhythm guitar playing in blues. Below we'll find three different variations on the chord patterns. To apply these to our 12-bar progressions, simply plug in the chord pattern over the appropriate chord in the progression.

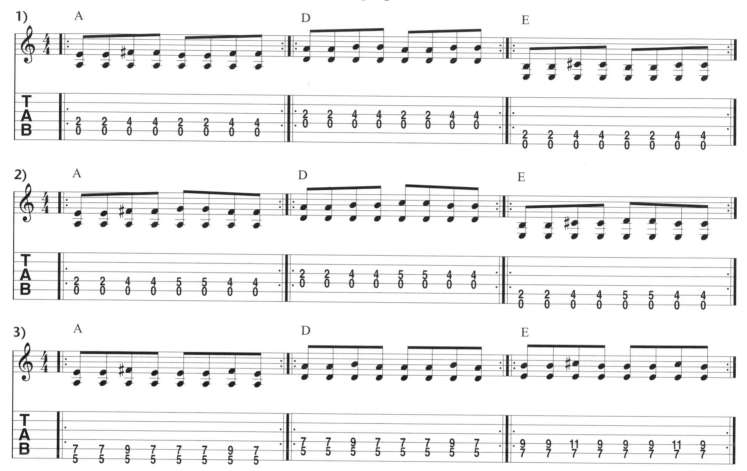

One-Note Patterns

Another common variation in blues rhythm is the *one-note* riffing style. Here are two different possibilities to that approach.

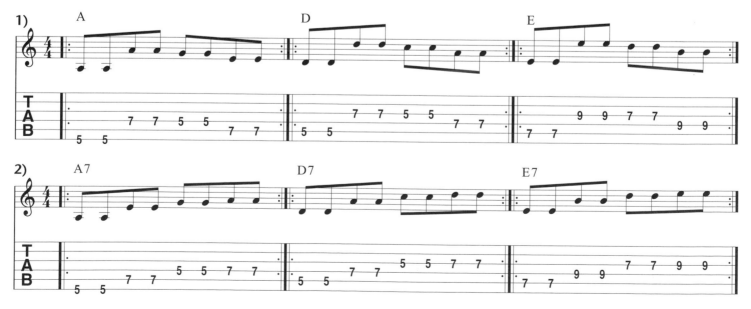

Finally, we see two examples of the *full-chord* approach to blues rhythm.

Full-Chord Patterns

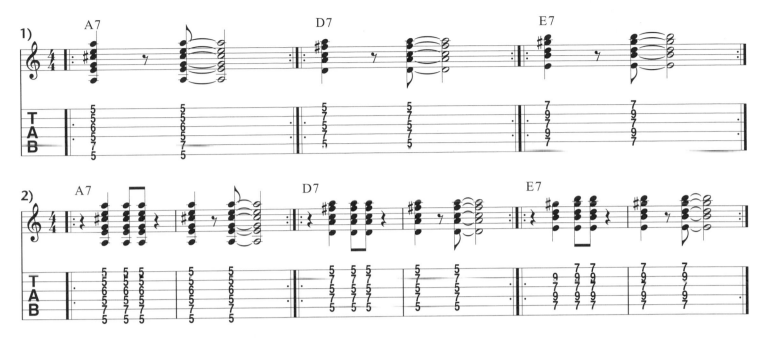

IMPROVISING CONCEPTS

A Minor Pentatonic over Entire Blues Progression

The easiest and probably the most common scale to use for the blues progression is the minor pentatonic built off the I chord. Even if this is not the "correct" scale for the dominant chords (because dominant chords have a major 3rd, while the minor pentatonic has a minor 3rd), it works very well, because we are so used to hearing this sound. Here we see how the scale degrees of the pentatonic function over the different chords in a blues in A.

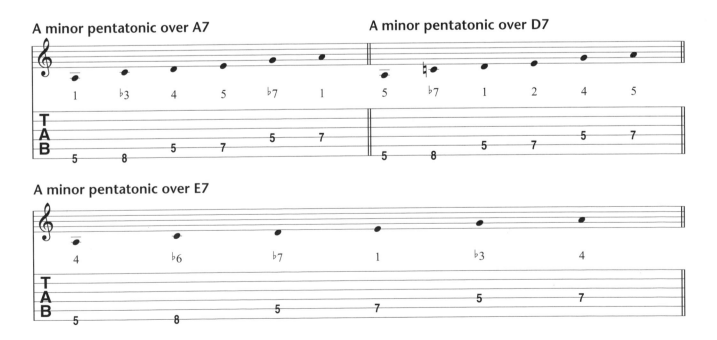

Shifting Major and Minor Pentatonics over Each Chord

This approach to soloing is a bit more difficult than the previous. Here, you'll be using A major pentatonic over the I chord (A7) and A minor pentatonic over the IV chord (D) and V chord (E).

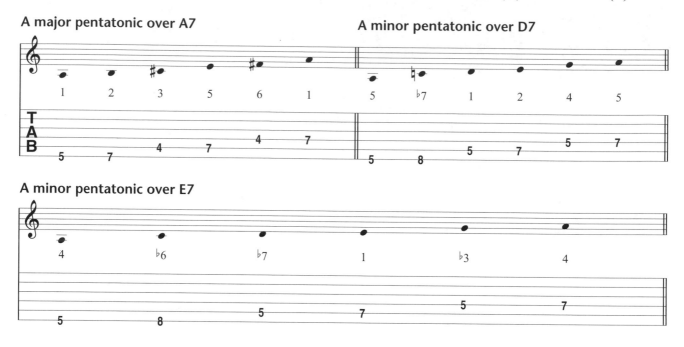

Shifting Major Pentatonics over Chords

Here, we're using a different major pentatonic over each chord. This will sound much brighter than the original method of using the minor pentatonic over the entire progression.

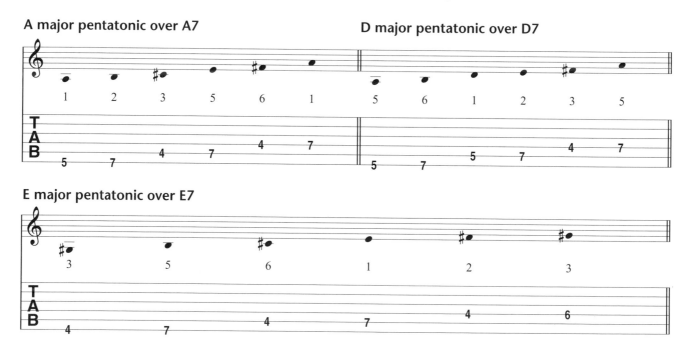

Note that these scales are not all shown in root position. Be sure to practice them in all their patterns over the entire neck.

Shifting Minor Pentatonics over Chords

Here, we're using A minor pentatonic over the A7, D minor pentatonic over the D7, and E minor pentatonic over the E7 chord. It is not common practice to use D minor pentatonic over D7 in an A blues. This is because the F note is too remote to the key of A and will have a tendency to sound sour.

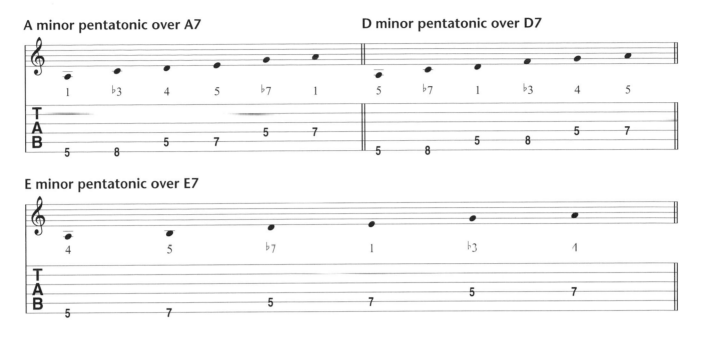

Mixolydian Scales

A more jazzy approach to the blues often times involves the use of the *Mixolydian scale* (or *mode*). A Mixolydian scale is the same as a major scale but with a lowered 7th degree. In A, the notes would be: A–B–C#–D– E–F#–G. Here we'll use a Mixolydian scale built off the root of each chord.

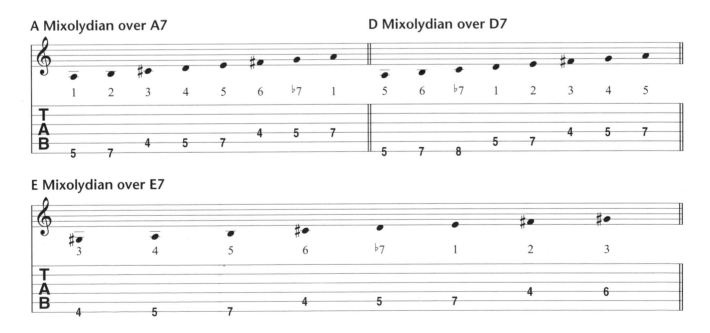

Blues Scales

Fittingly, another approach to soloing over a blues involves the use of the *blues scales*. Here we see that the minor and major blues scales can be combined into one scale. This new combined scale can be used over the entire progression; use your ear to judge when and when not to use certain notes.

A minor blues scale

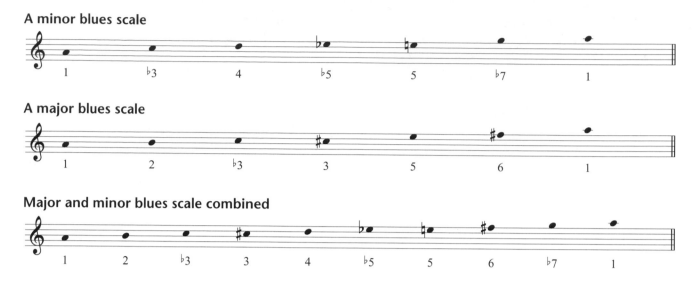

A major blues scale

Major and minor blues scale combined

HARMONY AND THEORY

Intervals

An *interval* is defined as the distance between two notes. We get the names of the intervals from counting the degrees of the major scale. An interval consists of two components: a number and a quality. We're going to look at the numbers here, and later we'll add the quality. Let's take a look at the intervals of a C major scale. The intervals will all be measured from the root note C.

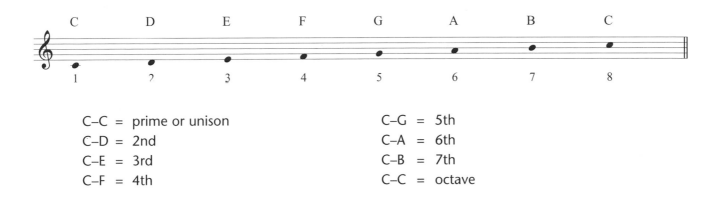

C–C	= prime or unison	C–G	= 5th
C–D	= 2nd	C–A	= 6th
C–E	= 3rd	C–B	= 7th
C–F	= 4th	C–C	= octave

We can determine the *number* of an interval between any two notes by simply counting through the notes of the C major scale, labeling the note from which you are measuring as 1. For example:

The interval from C to G is a 5th:

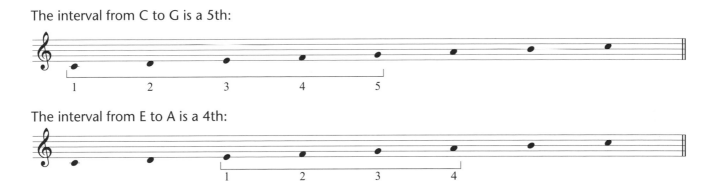

The interval from E to A is a 4th:

Now, let's see how many half steps make up the intervals that we learned in the notes from the C major scale. We commonly use the half step as the unit to measure intervals, because it's the smallest distance between two notes.

C to C (unison) = 0 half steps

C to D (2nd) = 2 half steps

C to E (3rd) = 4 half steps

C to F (4th) = 5 half steps

C to G (5th) = 7 half steps

C to A (6th) = 9 half steps

C to B (7th) = 11 half steps

C to C (octave) = 12 half steps

Perfect Intervals

The first type of quality in an interval that we're going to look at is perfect. The unison, the 4th, and the 5th intervals in a major scale are known as *perfect intervals*. If you combine a perfect 4th and a perfect 5th, you end up with an octave.

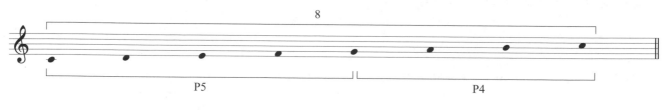

The Tritone

The *tritone* is a special case in intervals. It divides the octave exactly in half. In terms of intervals, it is either described as an *augmented 4th* or a *diminished 5th*. It consists of six half steps or three whole steps.

RHYTHM CONCEPTS

Rhythm Pyramids

Below, we'll find a *binary rhythm pyramid*. This is a convenient way of seeing how the largest rhythmic value (the whole note) can be continually divided in half. The numbers above the staff represent how these rhythms are typically counted. (The plus sign is read as "and" when counting.)

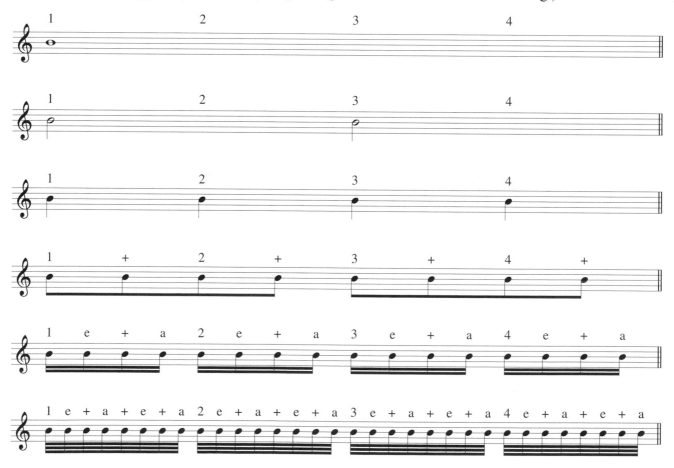

Here we see a *ternary rhythm pyramid*. This shows how the whole note can continually be divided in three.

(Count in eight-note subdivisions)

(Count in eight-note subdivisions)

Rhythm Exercise 7

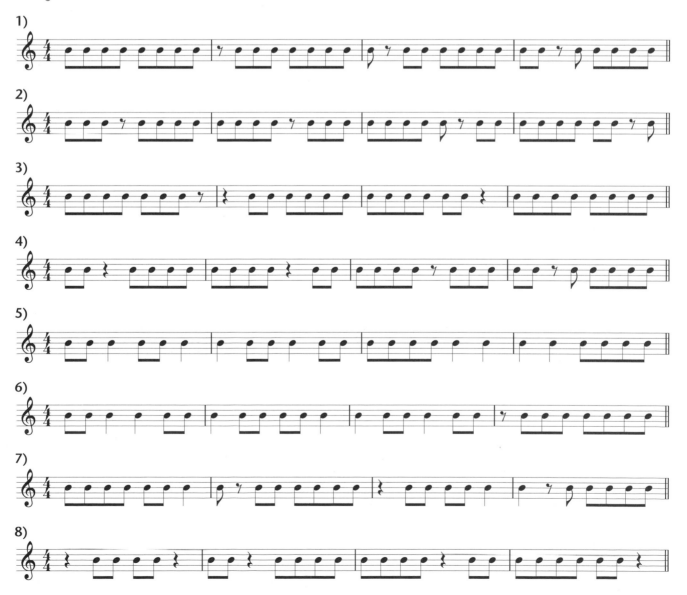

Rhythm Exercise 8

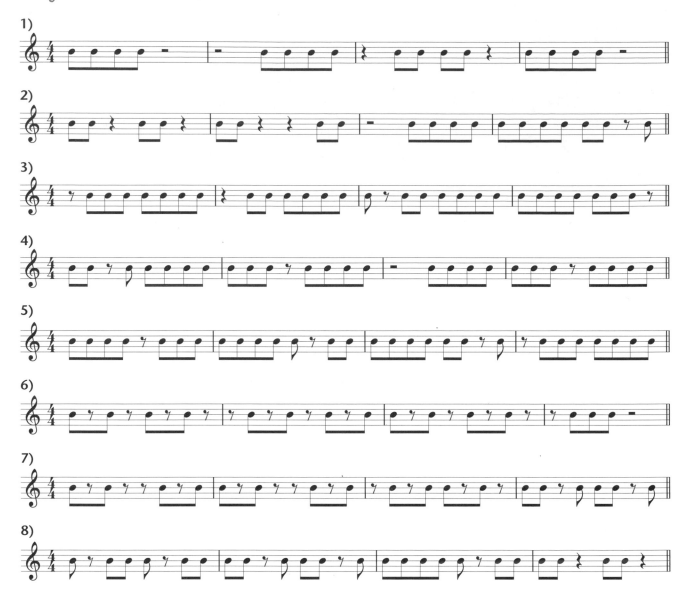

7th chords

Here we'll learn voicings for several different 7th chords built off the sixth, fifth, and fourth strings.

1) Root on 6th string

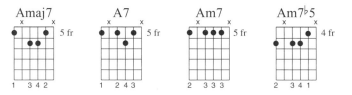

2) Root on 5th string

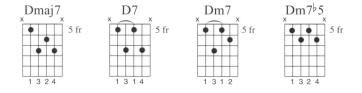

50

3) Root on 4th string

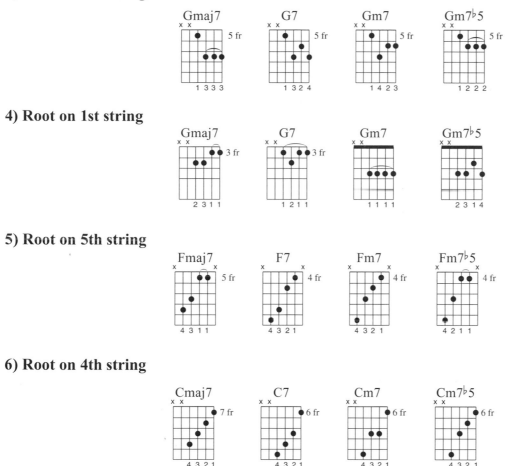

4) Root on 1st string

5) Root on 5th string

6) Root on 4th string

SIGHT-READING

Here we see the F major scale (remember this key has one flat, B♭) in first position.

F G A B♭ C D E F G A B♭ C D E F

The open strings can still be used as reference notes.

Write the name of each note underneath the staff:

Sight-Reading Exercise 7

F major, first position

Sight-Reading Exercise 8

F major, first position

SCALES AND TECHNIQUES

Major Scales

Now we're going to learn five patterns for the C major scale.

🔊 Track 10

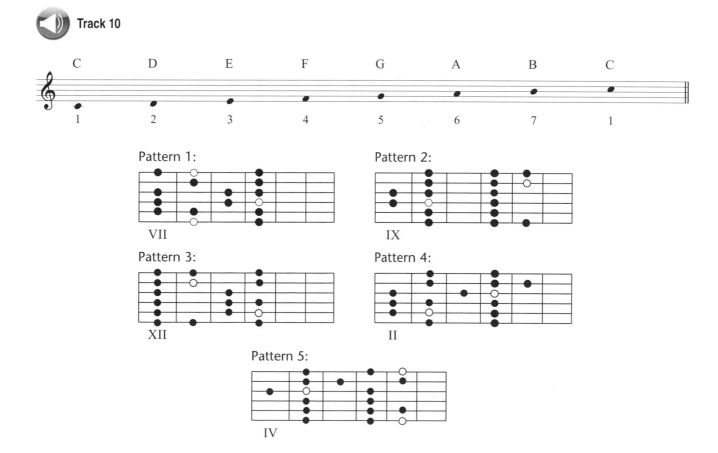

Minor Scales

Track 11

And now we see five patterns for the A minor scale (the relative minor of C major).

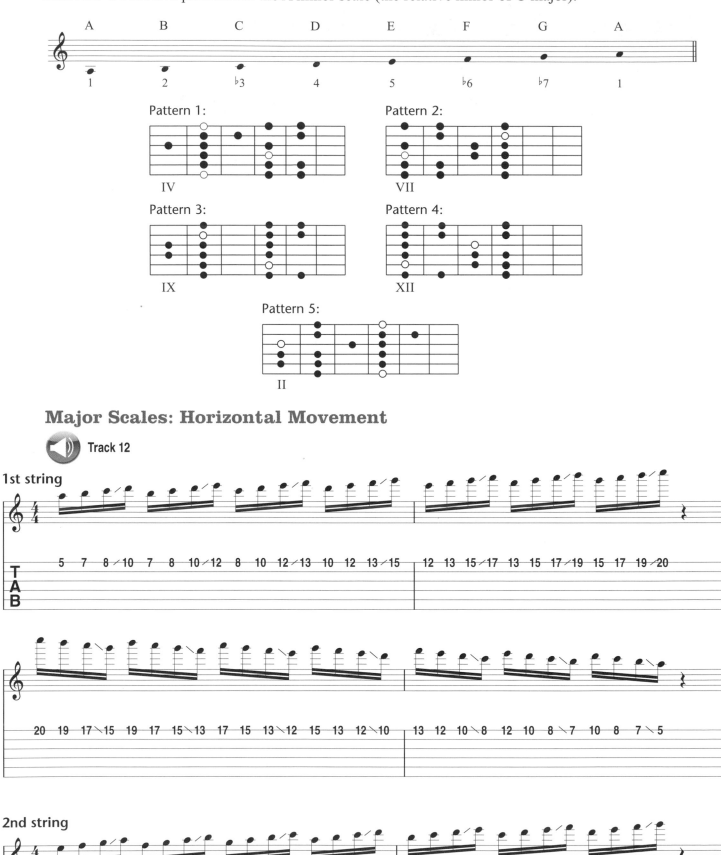

Major Scales: Horizontal Movement

Track 12

20 18 17＼15 18 17 15＼13 17 15 13＼12 15 13 12＼10 | 13 12 10＼8 12 10 8＼6 10 8 6＼5

3rd string

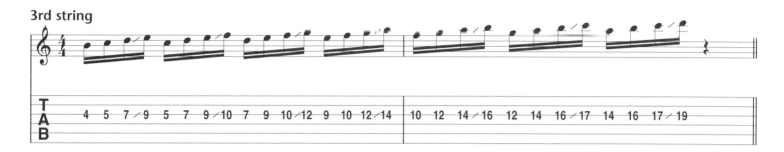

4 5 7／9 5 7 9／10 7 9 10／12 9 10 12／14 | 10 12 14／16 12 14 16／17 14 16 17／19

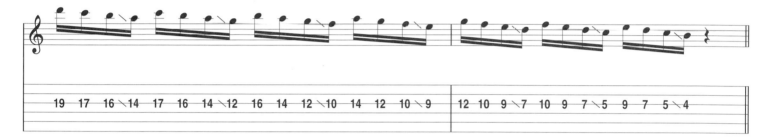

19 17 16＼14 17 16 14＼12 16 14 12＼10 14 12 10＼9 | 12 10 9＼7 10 9 7＼5 9 7 5＼4

4th string

5 7 9／10 7 9 10／12 9 10 12／14 10 12 14／15 | 12 14 15／17 14 15 17／19 15 17 19／21

21 19 17＼15 19 17 15＼14 17 15 14＼12 15 14 12＼10 | 14 12 10＼9 12 10 9＼7 10 9 7＼5

5th string

5 7 8／10 7 8 10／12 8 10 12／14 10 12 14／15 | 12 14 15／17 14 15 17／19 15 17 19／20

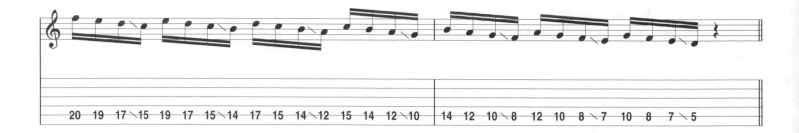

6th string

Interval Workout: C Major

In these exercises, you're going to become familiar with all the intervals of the C major scale.

🔊 Track 13

Thirds

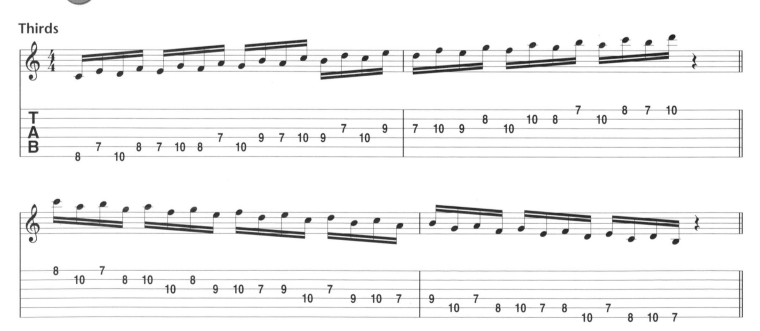

Fourths

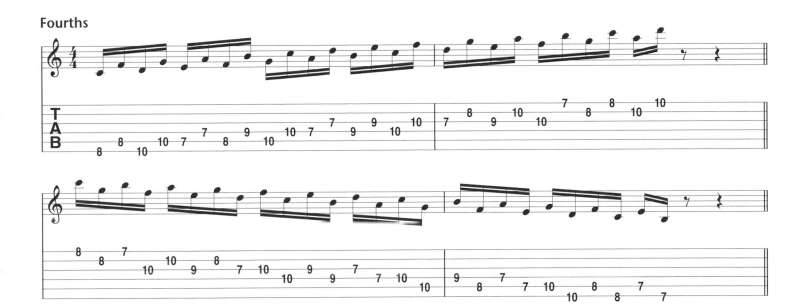

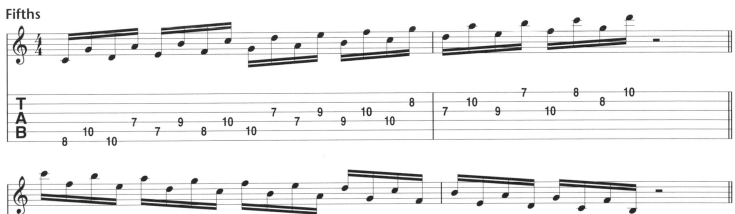

Fifths

Sixths

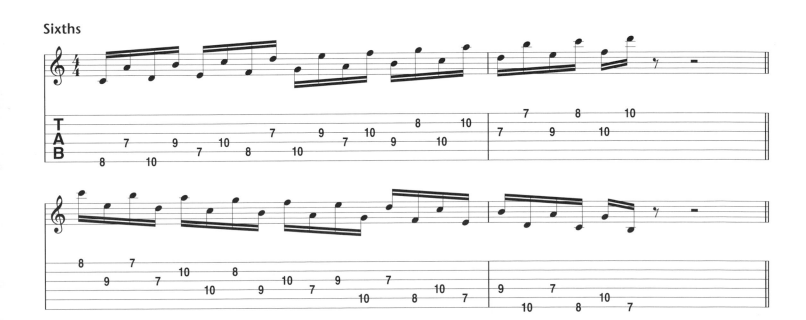

Sevenths

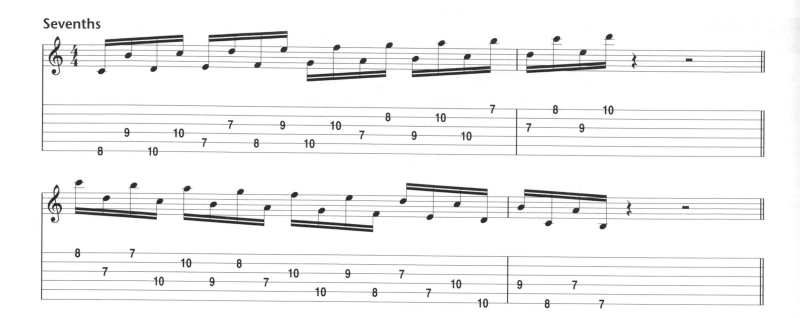

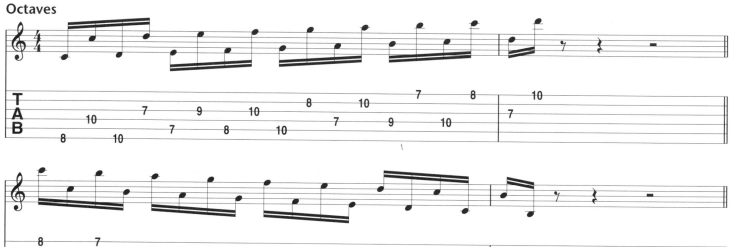

Octaves

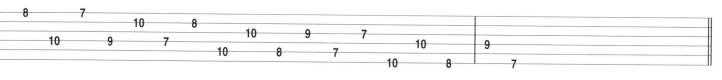

LESSON 2

HARMONY AND THEORY

Intervals II

In the last lesson, we learned about one component of intervals: the number. Now we're going to learn the other component: the *quality*. An interval may be one of five different qualities: major, minor, augmented, diminished, or perfect. While it may seem as though memorization is the only way to learn these, there are several formulas you should notice to expedite the learning of these.

1) A minor interval is always one half step smaller than its corresponding major interval.

2) A diminished interval is always one half step smaller than a perfect interval.

3) An augmented interval is always one half step larger than a perfect (or sometimes major) interval.

The following table shows all the intervals within one octave, as measured from the note C. Notice the above formulas at work.

Notes	Interval		Half Steps
C – C	perfect unison	1	0
C – D♭	minor second	♭2	1
C – D	major second	2	2
C – D♯	augmented second	♯2	3
C – E♭	minor third	♭3	3
C – E	major third	3	4
C – F	perfect fourth	4	5
C – F♯	augmented fourth	♯4	6
C – G♭	diminished fifth	♭5	6
C – G	perfect fifth	5	7
C – G♯	augmented fifth	♯5	8
C – A♭	minor sixth	♭6	8
C – A	major sixth	6	9
C – B♭	minor seventh	♭7	10
C – B	major seventh	7	11
C – C	octave	8	12

Compound Intervals

So far we've concentrated on intervals within one octave. But intervals that span more than an octave can also be named. These are called *compound intervals*. To name compound intervals, simply continue numbering the scale degrees past the octave. We'll use the note C again as the starting point. If the octave (C) is 8, then we continue with 9 for the note D and so on. This is illustrated below:

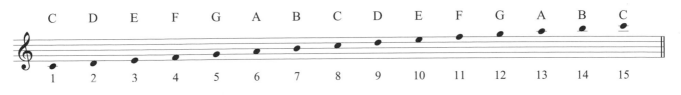

The following table shows all the intervals above one octave, as measured from the note C. As it is not common to number intervals higher than 13ths, the table stops there.

Notes	Interval		Half Steps
C – C	octave	8	12
C – D♭	minor ninth	♭9	13
C – D	major ninth	9	14
C – D♯	augmented ninth	♯9	15
C – E♭	minor tenth	♭10	15
C – E	major tenth	10	16
C – F	eleventh	11	17
C – F♯	augmented eleventh	♯11	18
C – G♭	diminished twelfth	♭12	18
C – G	twelfth	12	19
C – G♯	augmented twelfth	♯12	20
C – A♭	minor thirteenth	♭13	20
C – A	major thirteenth	13	21

Complementary Intervals

We learned last lesson that if you combine a perfect 4th and a perfect 5th you end up with an octave. Two intervals that form an octave when combined are known as *complementary intervals*. Below we'll see several more examples of complementary intervals:

minor second + major seventh = octave

major second + minor seventh = octave

minor third + major sixth = octave

major third + minor sixth = octave

tritone + tritone = octave

Interval Fingerings

Now that we've learned all these intervals, let's see what they look like on the guitar. We'll be using the note A as a reference this time. The chord charts below will demonstrate several ways to play each interval within one octave.

minor 2nd:

major 2nd:

minor 3rd:

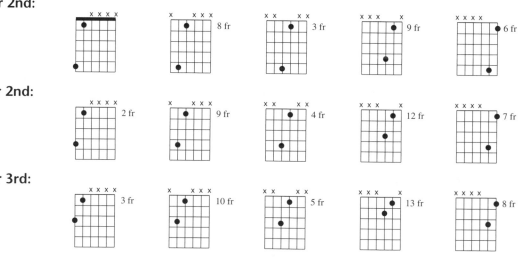

major 3rd:

perfect 4th:

perfect 5th:

diminished 5th:

minor 6th:

major 6th:

minor 7th:

major 7th:

octave:

RHYTHM CONCEPTS

Rhythm Pyramid Exercises

Use a metronome when playing this exercise. Start slow, using a tempo that allows you to play sixteenth notes easily. Repeat each rhythm first, and then try to play through the whole exercise with no repeats. This exercise makes use of binary rhythms.

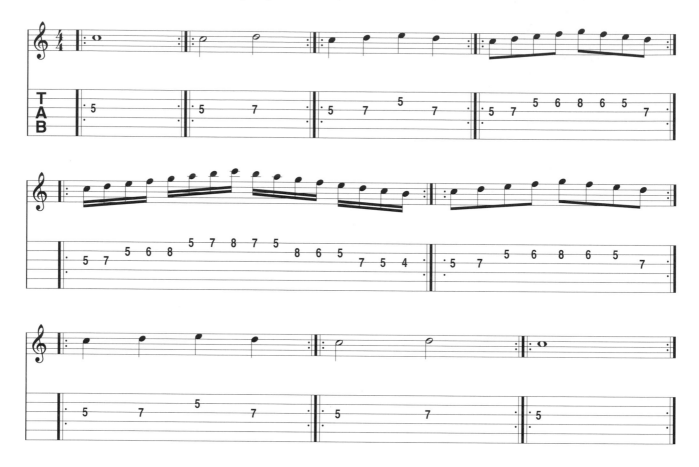

Now we see the same exercise applied to ternary rhythms.

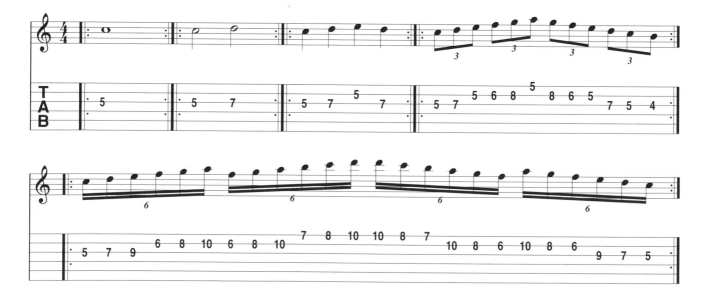

Rhythm Exercise 9

Rhythm Exercise 10

6th Chords

Here we'll learn several voicings for major and minor 6th chords.

1) Major 6th chords:

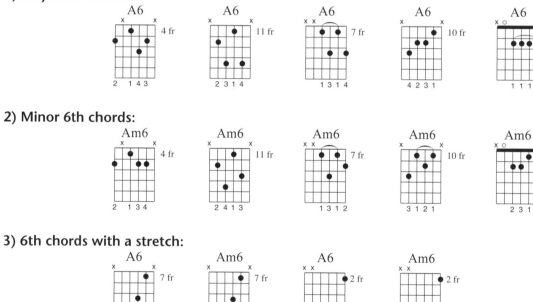

2) Minor 6th chords:

3) 6th chords with a stretch:

SIGHT-READING

Here we see the G major scale (one sharp: F♯) in first position.

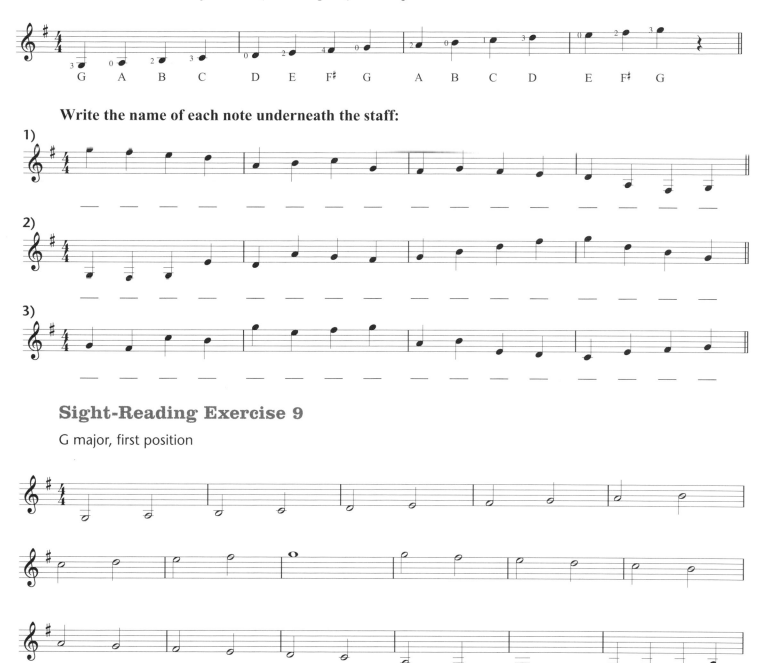

Write the name of each note underneath the staff:

1)

2)

3)

Sight-Reading Exercise 9

G major, first position

Sight-Reading Exercise 10

G major, first position

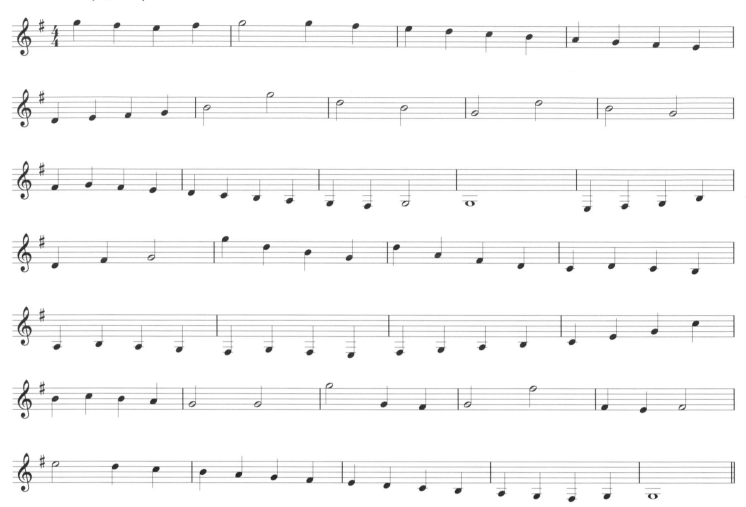

SCALES AND TECHNIQUES

Alternate Picking

Alternate picking is the most common of the picking techniques. This technique alternates downstrokes and upstrokes consistently in the right hand. It's important to note that, when playing long sixteenth-note lines, even when you rest for a sixteenth note you should still move the pick as though you were picking a note. This is sometimes called a "ghost stroke." The reason for this is that it enables you to keep the downstrokes on the downbeats throughout the phrase, therefore making it easier to keep your place in the phrase. These are indicated below by picking marks in parentheses.

 Track 14

A minor scale

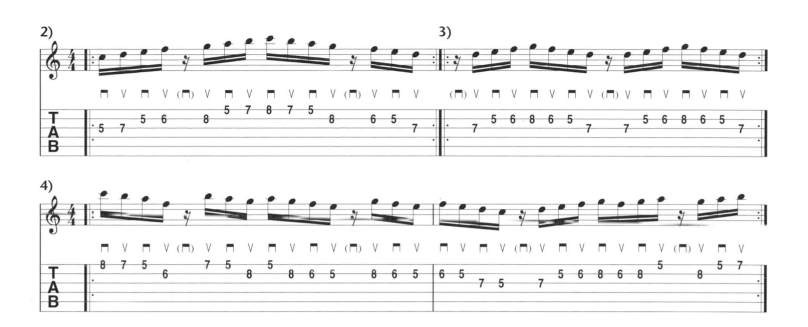

Repeating Patterns

Here we see some *repeating patterns* designed to strengthen your alternate picking skills. Continue to use strict alternate picking.

 Track 15

1) A minor

2) E minor

3) E minor

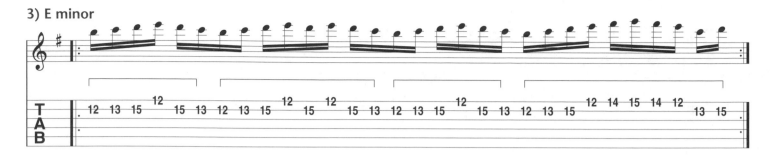

4) E minor

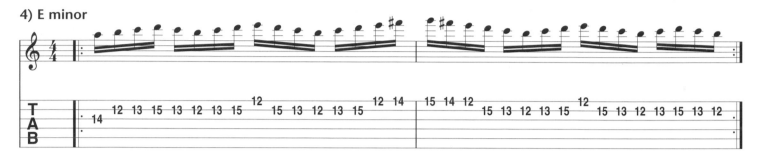

5) A minor   6) A minor

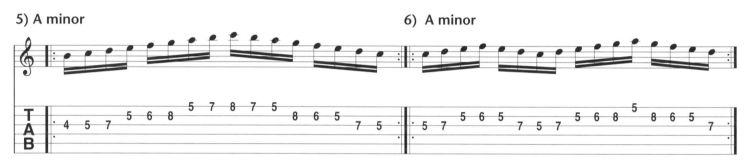

7) A minor   8) A minor

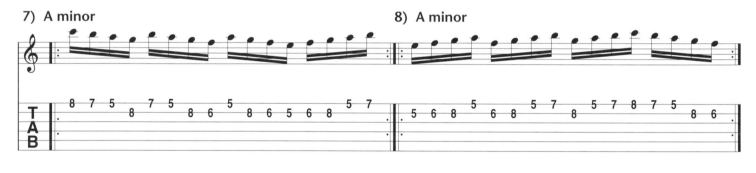

9) A minor: single string

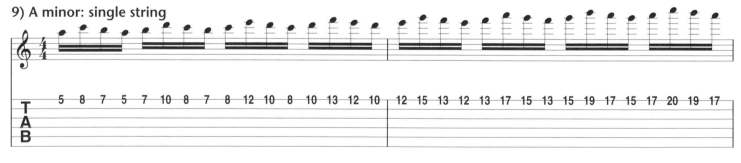

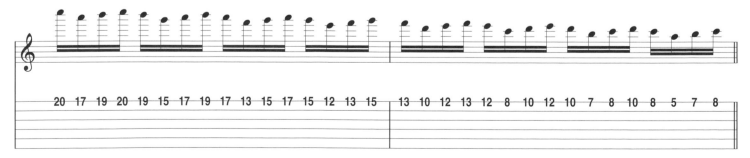

10)

```
8  5  7  8  10  7  8  10  12  8  10  12  13  10  12  13 | 15  12  13  15  17  13  15  17  19  15  17  19  20  17  19  20
```

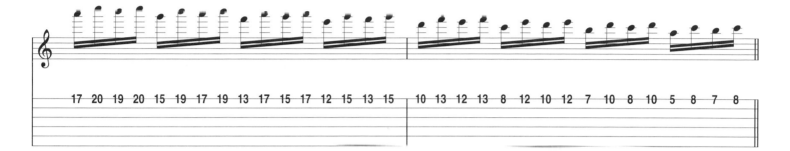

```
17  20  19  20  15  19  17  19  13  17  15  17  12  15  13  15 | 10  13  12  13  8  12  10  12  7  10  8  10  5  8  7  8
```

11) A minor with string skipping

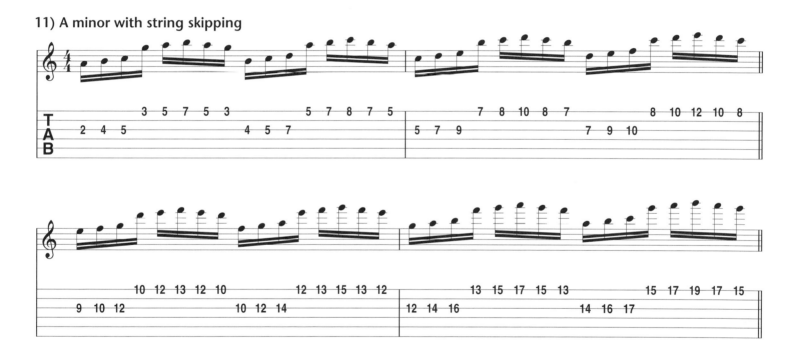

```
            3  5  7  5  3          5  7  8  7  5  |          7  8  10  8  7          8  10  12  10  8
2  4  5                  4  5  7           |  5  7  9                  7  9  10
```

```
        10  12  13  12  10          12  13  15  13  12  |          13  15  17  15  13          15  17  19  17  15
9  10  12                   10  12  14              |  12  14  16                  14  16  17
```

Pedal Tone Licks

A *pedal tone* involves the repeated use of one or more notes in alteration with other notes. It's a very popular device in classical music. Below we'll find several examples of pedal tone ideas. All of these examples will be derived from the E minor scale.

Track 16

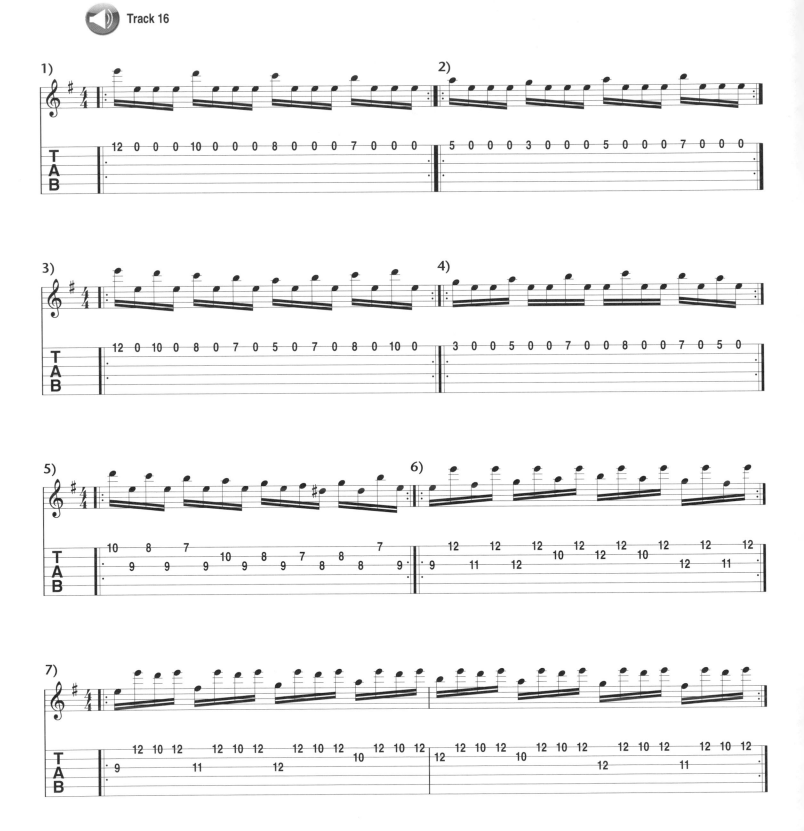

HARMONY AND THEORY

Circle of Fifths

The *circle of fifths* provides a convenient visual method for memorizing the key signatures for all the keys. Notice that if you start and the top and move to the right, it progresses in 5ths. If you move to the left, however, you progress in 4ths. There are a few other patterns you should notice to make the memorization easier.

1) As you move through the sharp keys, each new key carries all the sharps of the previous key and adds its own new one. This new sharp is the *leading tone* of that key. A leading tone is the 7th scale degree of a major scale.

2) As you move through the flat keys, you also add a new flat with every key. The flats, though, are *not* leading tones. You can think of them as signaling which new key is next. For example, in the key of B♭, we see B♭ and E♭. E♭ is the next key in the circle after B♭.

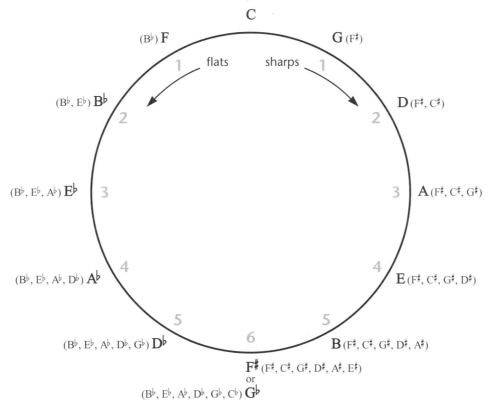

Relative Minors

We've learned the key signatures for all the major keys, but what about songs that begin and end on a minor chord? There are certainly songs that are in the key of A minor, D minor, etc. This is where the concept of the *relative minor* comes in. Every major key has a relative minor key, and they share the same key signature. The way we find a relative minor key is by locating the 6th degree of the major scale. For instance, in the key of C, we can determine that A is the relative minor by counting through the scale: C(1)–D(2)–E(3)–F(4)–G(5)–A(6). Below we'll find all twelve major keys and their relative minors:

	sharp keys					
major	C	G	D	A	E	B
relative minor	A	E	B	F♯	C♯	G♯

	flat keys					
major	F	B♭	E♭	A♭	D♭	G♭
relative minor	D	G	C	F	B♭	E♭

RHYTHM CONCEPTS

Muted Strums

Muting the strings lightly with your left hand while strumming can produce a percussive sound that can be used for a nice rhythmic effect. In the following exercises, make sure to use a metronome so your time is steady. The fifth example is a rhythm pyramid exercise that includes both binary and ternary rhythms.

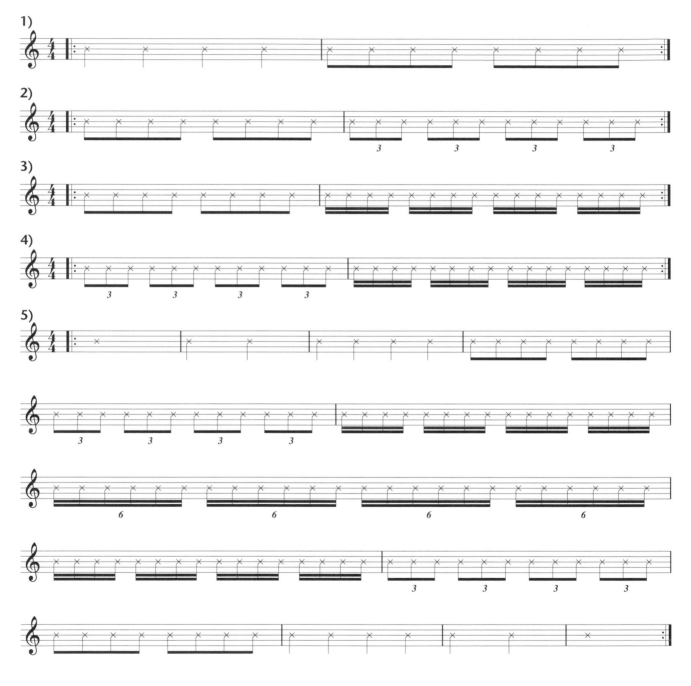

Rhythm Exercise 11

72

Rhythm Exercise 12

Diminished 7th Chords

Here we'll learn several voicings for *diminished 7th chords*. These chord shapes are unique in that they are symmetrical. This means that they can be repeated every minor 3rd.

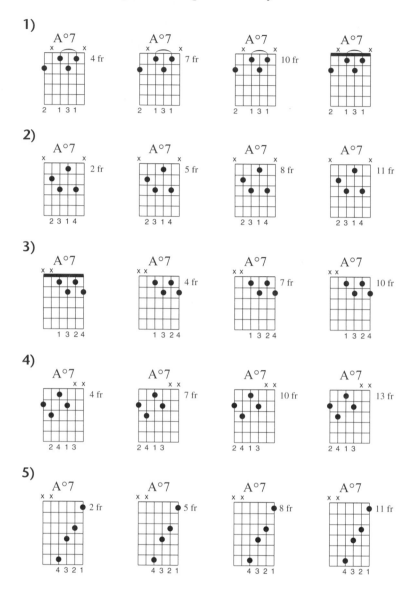

SIGHT-READING

Sight-Reading Exercise 11

F major, first position

Sight-Reading Exercise 12

G major, first position

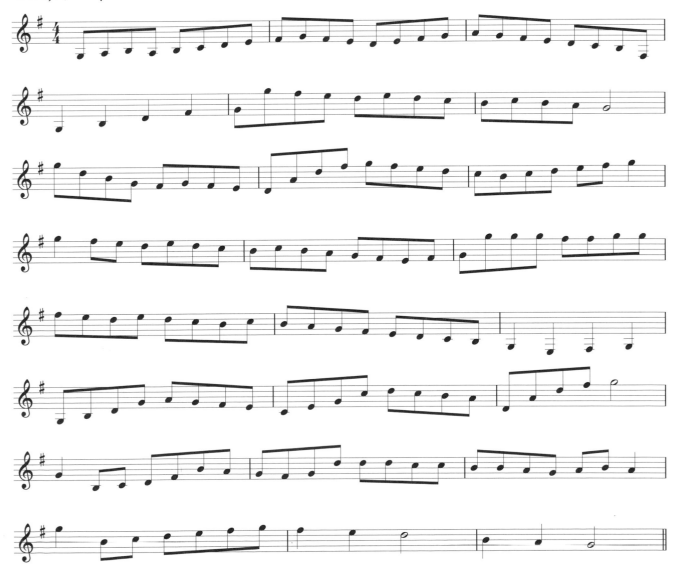

SCALES AND TECHNIQUES

Here we're going to take a closer look at some of the techniques we've seen thus far.

Bending

Bending is a technique that is very common in today's guitar playing. You can hear a lot of bends in blues or rock songs especially. Bending is not quite as easy as some people make it look, however. You have to be very aware of how far to bend the string, or it will sound out of tune. Usually, you want to bend a note to another note in the same scale or key. How far you bend a note depends on the scale that you are playing. The most common types of bends are whole-step bends, half-step bends, and quarter-step bends (also called "blues bends"). Much larger bends are possible though; some players bend strings as far as two-and-a-half steps or more! Let's look at some examples.

The first bend below is a whole step. Remember to check your pitch against the E note on the second string, fifth fret. Also remember to use your first and second fingers behind your third finger when bending for support. The second bend is a quarter step. This bend is not quite a half step and is used mainly to give a slight blues inflection to the note. The last bend is a half step. Again, you can check your target pitch (C) against the second string, first fret to make sure you're in tune. Generally speaking, when bending the three highest strings you should push them up (toward the ceiling) when bending; the three lower strings are usually pulled down (toward the floor).

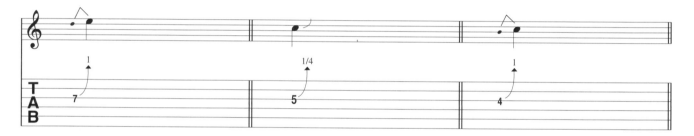

Here are some typical blues licks that make extensive use of bends. All of the examples are in A minor.

Track 17

76

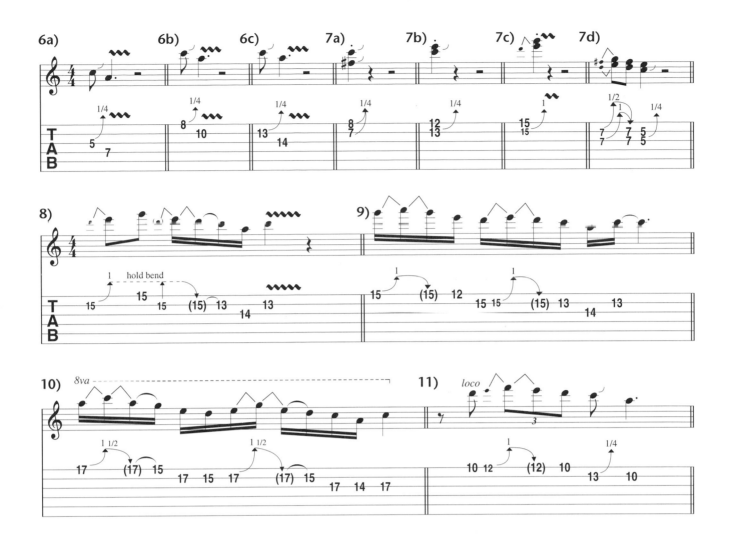

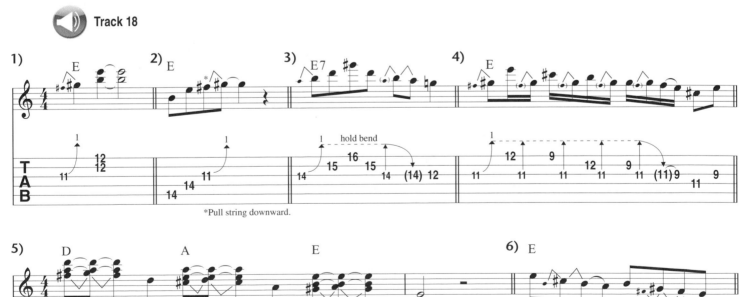

Now let's look at some examples of *country-style bends.* In these examples, I use a technique called *hybrid* picking. This means that I use both the pick and fingers in my right hand to pluck the strings. The technique involves pulling the higher strings with your right-hand fingers and allowing them to snap against the fretboard. Really pop them good to get that country sound.

Track 18

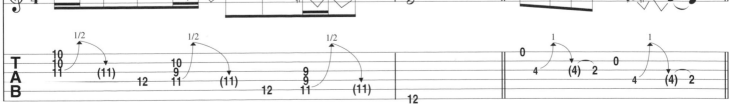

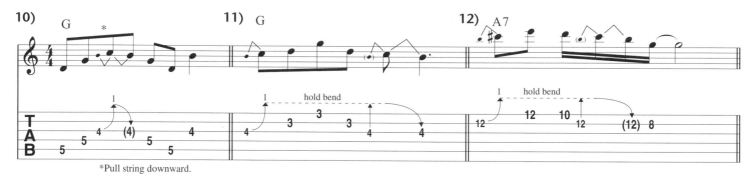

*Pull string downward.

Vibrato

Vibrato is a subtle (or sometimes not so subtle) expressive technique that involves the rapid slight fluctuation in pitch on a sustained note. On guitar, this involves slightly bending and releasing the note repeatedly as you hold it out. In order to gain control over your vibrato, it's good to practice to a metronome. Try the following exercises:

1) With your first finger on the fifth fret, third string (C), vibrato the note in an eight-note rhythm.

2) Now try a triplet rhythm with your third finger on the seventh fret, third string (D).

Practice these exercises on all strings with all of your fingers. For a subtle vibrato, bend the string more slightly, such as a quarter step. For a more intense vibrato, bend the string a half or whole step.

There are three different kinds of vibrato techniques that most guitarists use:

1) Rock vibrato: Bend the note up and release it to the original note, repeating continuously. In this method, the intonation goes sharp and back to normal.

2) Classical vibrato: Instead of bending the note up and down, you tug back and forth laterally along the length of the guitar neck. This method will make the intonation go sharp and flat.

3) Circular vibrato: This is essentially a combination of the two ways described above.

Experiment with these various types and see which ones feel and sound best to you.

Slides

Sliding is another very common tool that guitarists use to play with expression. Like bending and vibrato, it has its own sound and is used very often by a lot of great guitarists. Practice these examples and transpose them in different keys. Listen to your favorite solos and pay attention to how players use slides in their solos.

Track 19

1) A minor pentonic

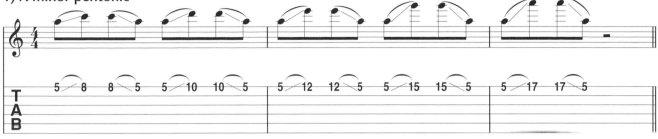

```
5 - 8    8 - 5    5 - 10   10 - 5    5 - 12   12 - 5    5 - 15   15 - 5    5 - 17   17 - 5
```

2) A minor pentonic

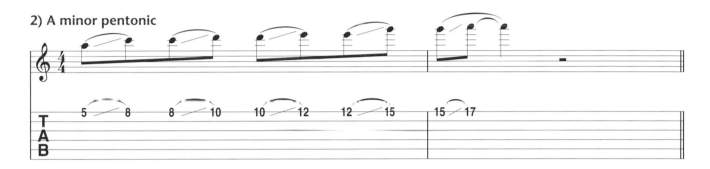

```
5 - 8    8 - 10   10 - 12   12 - 15   15 - 17
```

3) Am7 arpeggio   **Amaj7 arpeggio**

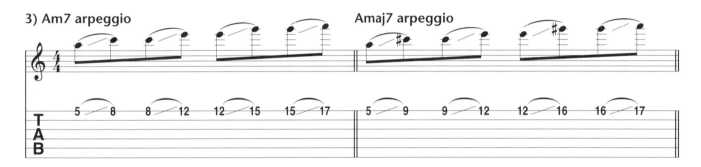

```
5 - 8    8 - 12   12 - 15   15 - 17    5 - 9    9 - 12   12 - 16   16 - 17
```

3) A7 arpeggio   **Am7♭5 arpeggio**

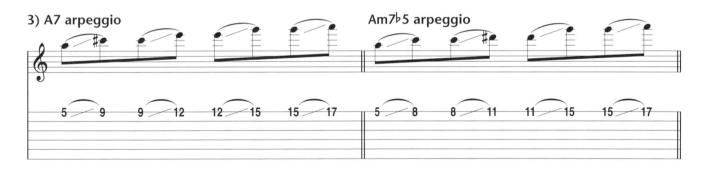

```
5 - 9    9 - 12   12 - 15   15 - 17    5 - 8    8 - 11   11 - 15   15 - 17
```

4) A minor lick

```
5 - 7    7 - 9    9 - 7    7 - 5    7 - 9    9 - 12   12 - 9    9 - 7    5
```

In these next two examples, the same phrases are played with bends and slides. Listen closely to the difference in sound.

Track 20

LESSON 4 • ROCK

PALM MUTING

The technique of *palm muting* involves resting your right palm near on the bridge as you strum, creating a choked, muffled sound. This is especially popular in heavier rock and metal styles.

In the following examples, use all downstrokes for the eighth notes to get the driving rock feel.

SIXTEENTH-NOTE RHYTHMS

Many times in rock and metal styles, you're required to play continuous *sixteenth-note rhythms.* Try to minimize the movement in your right hand to gain speed and stamina. Use alternate picking for all the examples below.

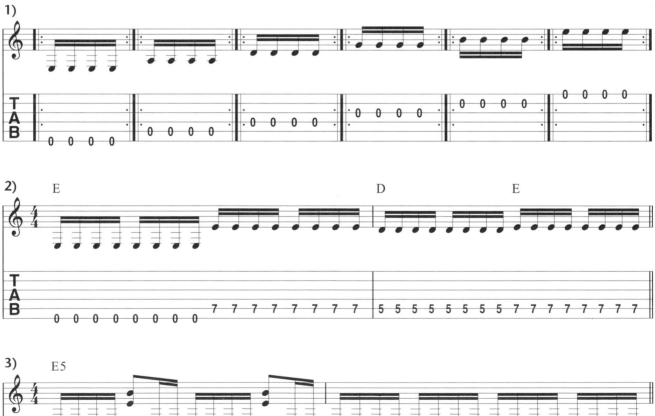

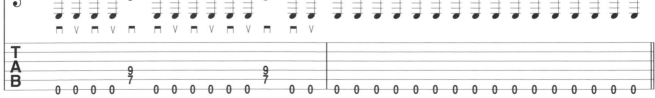

4)

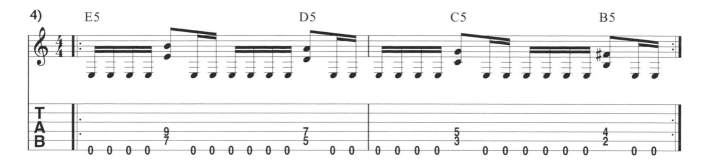

5)

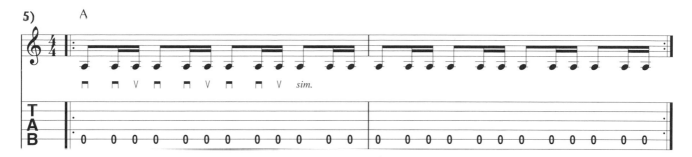

6)

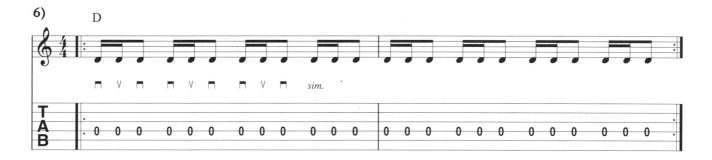

7)

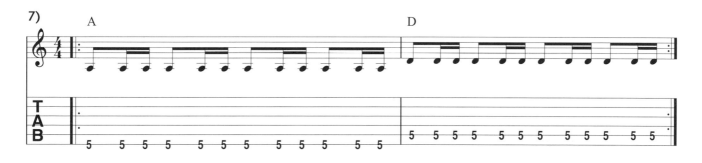

8)

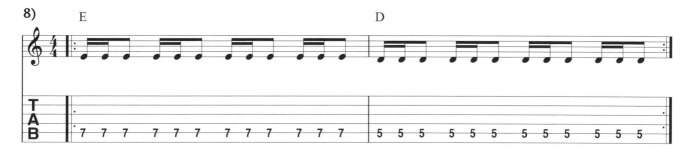

SCRATCH NOTES

We touched on this technique earlier in the book. It involves muting all the strings with your left hand. You can either lift up your left hand and lay it flat over the strings, or you can release the pressure of the chord that you are fretting.

OCTAVES

When playing octaves, it's very important to mute the strings that you are not playing to avoid excessive noise. This is accomplished by using the curvature of your first finger to lightly touch all the strings underneath it. Try the examples below.

1) D minor scale

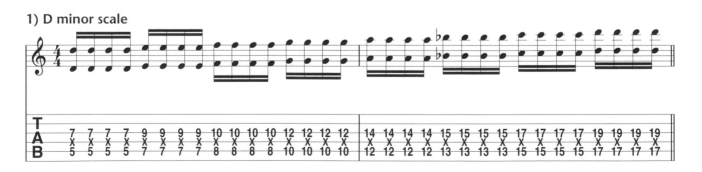

2) E minor

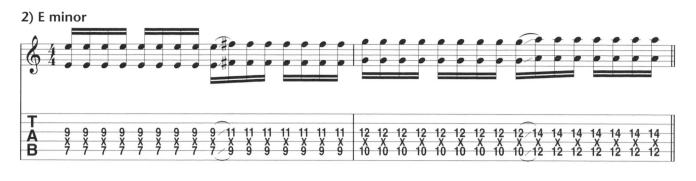

3) F minor

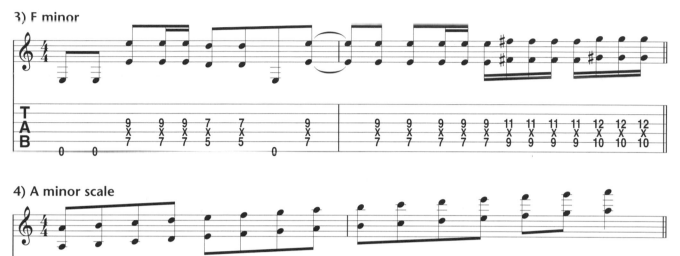

4) A minor scale

IMPROVISING CONCEPTS

As with many other styles, rock can be divided into many subcategories. Below is a general list of these and some basic guidelines to consider when improvising in these styles. We've already covered some of the techniques discussed; others will be covered at a later point in the book. You can use this as a reference when you're ready to start playing one of these styles.

1) Classic rock: We identify classic rock as mostly bands from the late sixties, seventies, and early eighties. Guitar players from that era mostly borrowed scales and licks from the blues. Try to use minor pentatonics and blues scales for soloing.

2) Southern rock: This style lies somewhere between country, blues, and rock. Use more major pentatonics and blues scales. Try some country licks with some distortion.

3) Eighties rock and metal: Use major and minor scales. Guitarists were more into practicing technique and used more sequences, arpeggios, scalar runs, etc.

4) Classical rock: This style, as the name implies, incorporates a classical influence into rock music. Try some major scale sequences or arpeggios. Borrow some chord progressions or cadences from classical pieces and harmonize them with arpeggios.

MISCELLANEOUS TECHNIQUES

Below we'll find a few techniques that are very commonly used in rock and blues styles. These examples will be in the key of A minor.

In this first example, we see how slides are often used to accent the first and last notes of a phrase. The amount of frets isn't crucial here; you're just going for an effect.

A *rake* is another technique used to accent or give weight to a note. This involves quickly "strumming" through several muted strings (muted with the palm of your right hand) on your way to a note. In the first example below, mute the fifth, fourth, and third strings with your right-hand palm, leaving the second string untouched. Quickly pick from the fifth string down through to the second string.

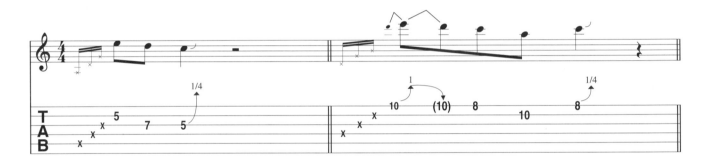

Pinch harmonics were used extensively in eighties metal. This technique involves allowing a portion of your thumb to touch the string as you pick. You'll probably need to experiment for a while to get the feel for it. Once you get the hang of it, however, you'll be able to get several different notes just by picking at different points along the string.

HARMONY AND THEORY

Triads

A *triad* is a chord that consists of three different notes. We build a triad by stacking two notes in 3rds above the root. In a C major triad, for example, we would stack a 3rd above the root note: C(1)–E(3). Next, we would stack another 3rd on top of that: C(1)–E(3)–G(5). So a C major triad would look like this: C–E–G. A triad always consists of a root, 3rd, and 5th. Below we'll find several examples of different types of triads.

As you can see, triads are usually easy to recognize because the three notes either fall on consecutive lines or consecutive spaces on the staff. Let's take a look again at our C major scale:

We're going to build a triad off of every note by stacking two notes in 3rds above it. If the first note is written on a line, we'll write the other two notes on the two lines above. If the first note is written in a space, we'll write them in the spaces above. Here we see all of the triads of the major scale:

After close examination of the intervals that make up these triads, we can determine that there are three different types of triads present: major, minor, and diminished. How did we know this? Let's take a detailed look at the construction of these three types of triads.

Major Triads

A *major triad* consists of a major 3rd and a perfect 5th above the root (1–3–5). The major triads in the C major scale are C, F, and G. Let's check this against a C major triad:

• From C to E, we should have a major 3rd (four half steps): C–C♯ (1), C♯–D (2), D–D♯ (3), D♯–E (4).

• From C to G, we should have a perfect 5th (seven half steps): C–C♯ (1), C♯–D (2), D–D♯ (3), D♯–E (4), E–F (5), F–F♯ (6), F♯–G (7). The F and G triads will also fit this formula.

Minor Triads

Next, we have the *minor triad*. A minor triad consists of a minor 3rd and a perfect 5th above the root (1–♭3–5). The minor triads in the C major scale are Dm, Em, and Am. Let's check the intervals of our Dm triad:

- From D to F, we should have a minor 3rd (three half steps): D–D♯ (1), D♯–E (2), E–F (3).

- From D to A, we should have a perfect 5th (seven half steps): D–D♯ (1), D♯–E (2), E–F (3), F–F♯ (4), F♯–G (5), G–G♯ (6), G♯–A (7). The Em and Am triads will also fit this formula.

Diminished Triads

The third type of triad we saw in the major scale was the *diminished triad*. This consists of a minor 3rd and a diminished 5th above the root (1–♭3–♭5). We only had one diminished triad: B°.

- From B to D, we should have a minor 3rd (three half steps): B–C (1), C–C♯ (2), C♯–D (3).

- From B to F, we should have a diminished 5th (six half steps): B–C (1), C–C♯ (2), C♯–D (3), D–D♯ (4), D♯–E (5), E–F (6).

So, we can determine that, in every major scale, the first, fourth, and fifth degrees will be major triads, the second, third, and sixth degrees will be minor triads, and the seventh degree will be a diminished triad. We can use Roman numerals to indicate this:

Augmented Triads

There is one more type of triad that is not present in the major scale. The *augmented triad* consists of a major 3rd plus an augmented 5th (1–3–♯5). Since this triad is not within the key, it will require an accidental. This triad is especially interesting because it consists of nothing but major 3rds. Therefore, if you were to move through the inversions of the chord on the same group of strings, the chord form would stay the same. Below we see a C augmented triad. Notice the symbol (+) that is used to denote augmented triads.

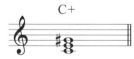

Let's check the intervals of this triad to make sure it fits the formula.

- From C to E, we should have a major 3rd. We know that we do from the C major triad above.

- From C to G♯, we should have an augmented 5th (eight half steps): C–C♯ (1), C♯–D (2), D–D♯ (3), D♯–E (4), E– F (5), F–F♯ (6), F♯–G (7), G–G♯ (8).

Now let's take a look at all four triad types with C as their root. Notice that we'll need to adjust the notes with accidentals in order to fit the interval formulas of each triad.

RHYTHM CONCEPTS

Time Signatures

So far, we've mainly worked with 4/4 time signatures. But there are other types of time signatures that you will encounter. They can be divided into basically three categories: even meters, compound meters, and odd meters.

Even Meters

The *even meter* is the most common type of time signature. These generally include all time signatures in which the beats are divided evenly or in multiples of two (binary). Some examples include 4/4, 2/4, 2/2, and 3/4. See below for examples:

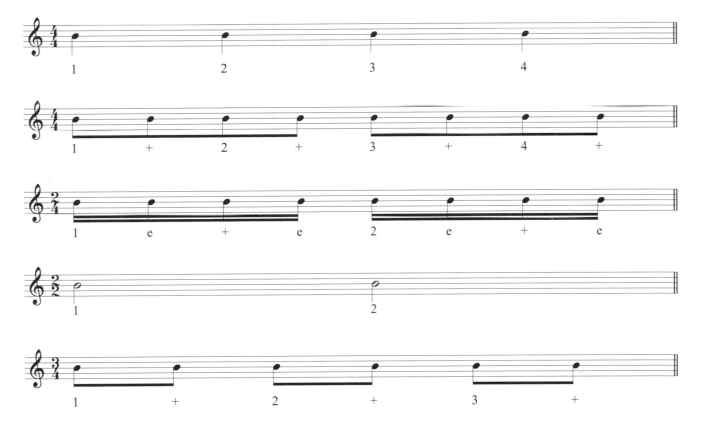

Compound Meters

A *compound meter* exists when the beats (or pulse, as we'll see) is divided into groups of three. Some examples include 6/8, 9/8, and 12/8. These are a bit more confusing than even meters. If we look at the components of a 6/8 time signature, for instance, we determine that the eighth note gets the beat and there are six eighth notes in a measure. However, in compound meters, three eighth notes are usually counted or perceived as one beat or "pulse." So a piece in 6/8 is usually counted: **1** - 2 - 3 - **4** - 5 - 6, **1** - 2 - 3 - **4** - 5 - 6, etc. See below:

Odd Meters

Odd meters are the result of essentially combining even and compound meters. Some examples of odd meters include 5/8, 7/8, 9/8, and 11/8. You may have noticed that 9/8 was listed as a compound meter as well. The only difference lies in how the nine eighth notes are grouped or counted. If they are grouped in three groups of three, then it is a compound meter. If they are grouped any other way, it is an odd meter. Let's take a look at some examples below:

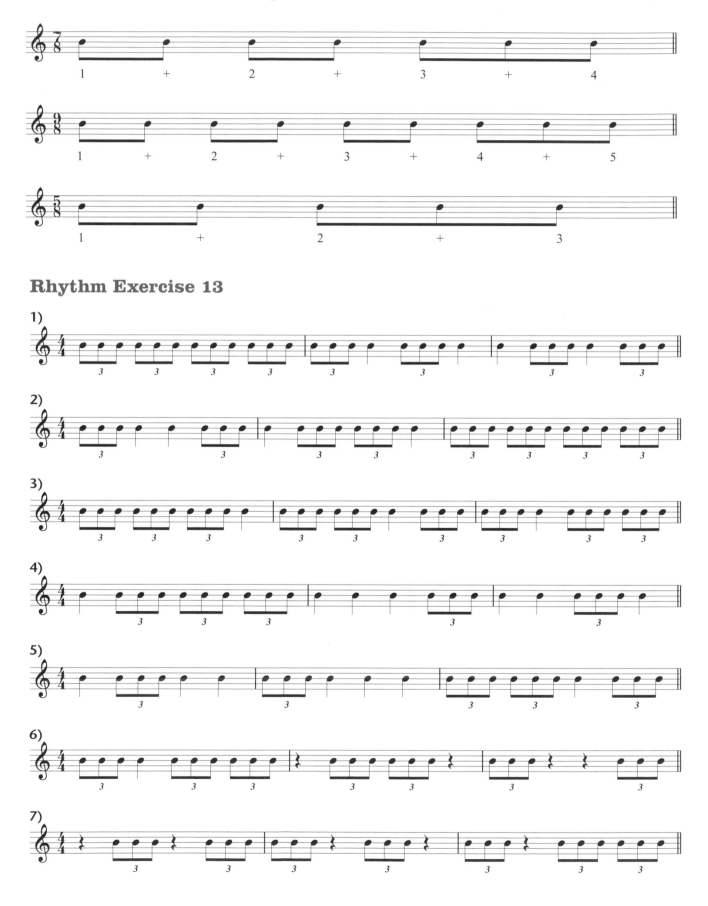

Rhythm Exercise 13

1)

2)

3)

4)

5)

6)

7)

Rhythm Exercise 14

Triads: Major and Minor

Here we're going to learn how to play the triads we learned on the guitar. Below we'll find twelve different voicings for G and twelve for Gm. Notice that the only difference between the two is the change from the note B in G to B♭ in Gm.

Major triads:

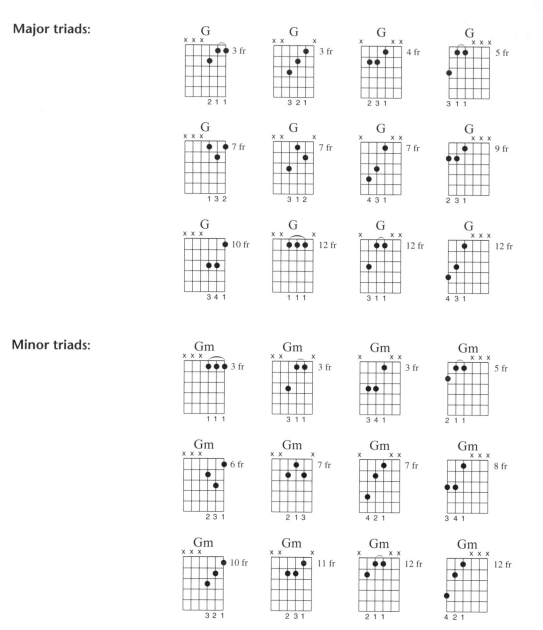

Minor triads:

SIGHT-READING

Let's move into second position for the C major scale now. The circled notes can act as your new reference notes. They stay the same in several sharp keys.

G A B C D E F G A B C D E F G A

Write the name of each note underneath the staff:

Sight-Reading Exercise 13

C major, second position

C major, second position

SCALES AND TECHNIQUES

Three-Note-per-String Scales/Modes

Scales arranged with three notes on each string are many times used in fast runs and licks. Their symmetry lays out logically on the guitar for both the fretting hand and the picking hand. Here we'll learn the seven *three-note-per-string* patterns for the C major scale. These seven different patterns each have their own name, and this is where we get *modes*. The seven modes are created by simply playing the notes of a major scale starting from each note of that scale. For instance, in C major, if you were to start on D and play to D you would have the second mode in C major: D Dorian. Below we'll find the seven modes of the C major scale. Remember to practice these in all keys.

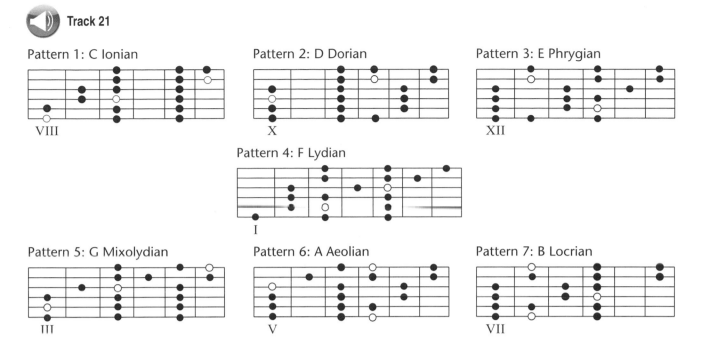

Pattern 1: C Ionian

Pattern 2: D Dorian

Pattern 3: E Phrygian

Pattern 4: F Lydian

Pattern 5: G Mixolydian

Pattern 6: A Aeolian

Pattern 7: B Locrian

You probably noticed that modes 1 and 6 (Ionian and Aeolian) go by two other names as well—the major scale and the minor scale! You already know the formulas for those two scales (see Chapter 1, Lesson 1 for a review), so let's take a look at the formulas for the remaining five modes:

Dorian: 1–2–♭3–4–5–6–♭7

Phrygian: 1–♭2–♭3–4–5–♭6–♭7

Lydian: 1–2–3–♯4–5–6–7

Mixolydian: 1–2–3–4–5–6–♭7

Locrian: 1–♭2–♭3–4–♭5–♭6–♭7

You can see how certain modes very closely resemble either the major or minor scale. The Dorian and Phrygian modes are only one note different from the minor scale, while the Lydian and Mixolydian modes are only one note different from the major scale.

Three-Note-per-String Sequences

It's very popular in rock styles to play sequences with these three-note-per-string shapes. Here we'll take a look at several different sequence ideas in scale pattern 1 of C major. Use strict alternate picking for these.

 Track 22

1a) Ascending group of 4 (1-2-3-4, 2-3-4-5, 3-4-5-6, 4-5-6-7, etc.)

1b) Descending group of 4 (4-3-2-1, 3-2-1-7, 2-1-7-6, 1-7-6-5, etc.)

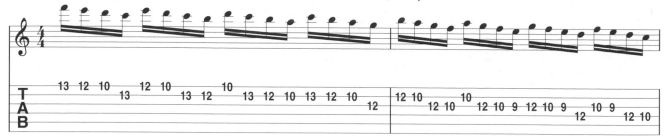

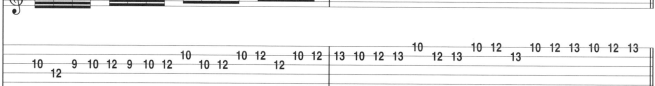

2a) Ascending group of 4 (3-1-2-3, 4-2-3-4, 5-3-4-5, 6-4-5-6, etc.)

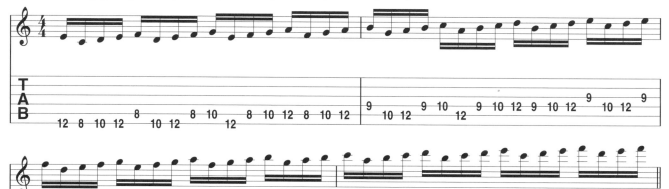

2b) Descending group of 4 (2-4-3-2, 1-3-2-1, 7-2-1-7, 6-1-7-6, etc.)

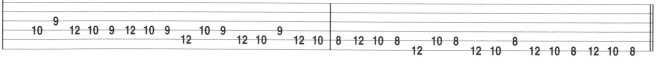

96

3a) Ascending group of 6 (1-2-3-4-3-2, 1-2-3-4-5-6, 4-5-6-7-6-5, 4-5-6-7-8-9, etc.)

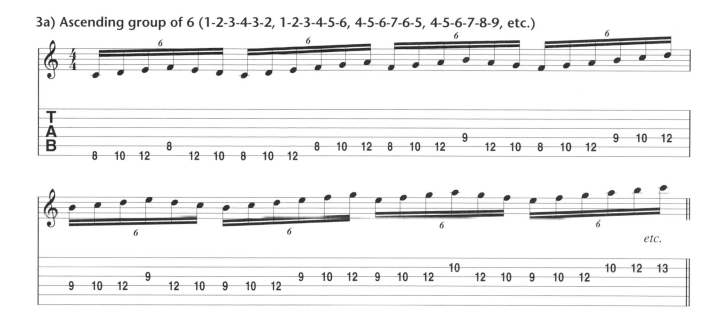

3b) Descending group of 6 (4-3-2-1-2-3, 4-3-2-1-7-6, 1-7-6-5-6-7, 1-7-6-5-4-3, etc.)

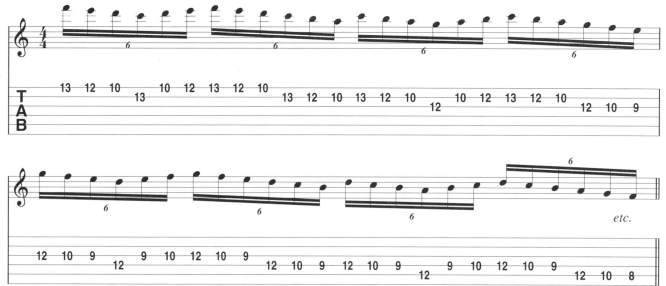

HARMONY AND THEORY

Triad Inversions

So far, all the triads that we have learned are in root position (1–3–5). This means that the root is always the lowest note of the triad. If you transpose the lowest note (root) up an octave, you get what we call a *first inversion* triad (3–5–1). Let's take a look at some first inversion triads from our C major scale:

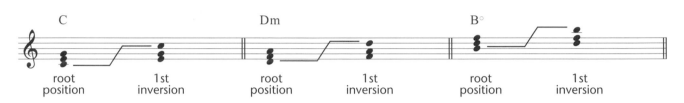

If we continue this process of taking the lowest note (now the 3rd) and transposing it up an octave, we end up with a *second inversion* triad (5–1–3). Let's take a look at some second inversion triads from our C major scale:

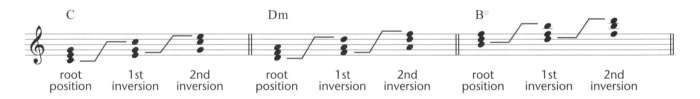

RHYTHM CONCEPTS

Dotted Notes

We learned earlier that a dot next to a note increases its value by 50 percent. Dotted notes are very similar to tied notes in this way, and it's certainly possible to write the same rhythm with both methods. This is demonstrated in the examples below. Each two-measure phrase would be read the same way.

There are times, however, when one method is preferred over another. The general rule, in a 4/4 time signature, is that you don't want to tie a note over the middle of the measure. In other words, you want the third beat to be visible. The examples below demonstrate this. The first measure of each two-measure phrase illustrates the undesirable method, while the second measure demonstrates how, by using ties, the middle of the measure becomes visible and the rhythm is therefore easier to read.

Rhythm Exercise 15

Rhythm Exercise 16

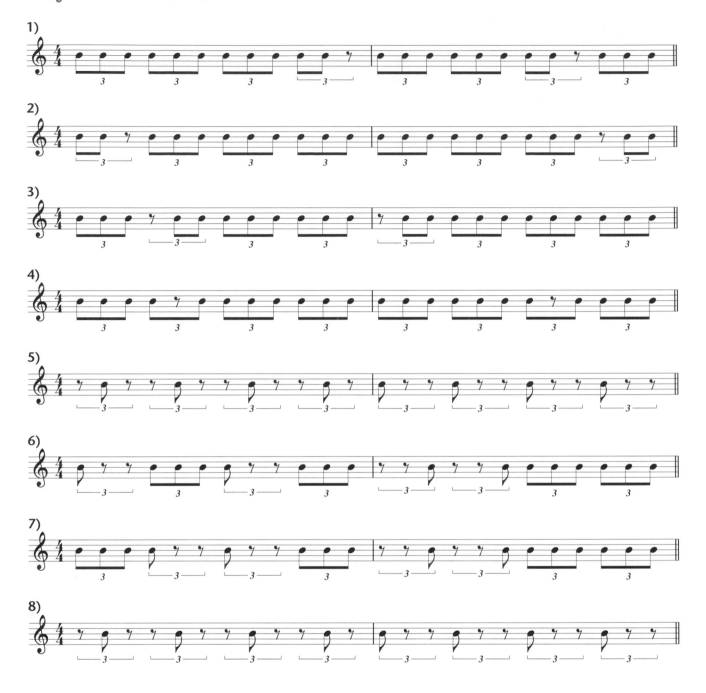

Triads: Diminished and Augmented

Diminished triads:

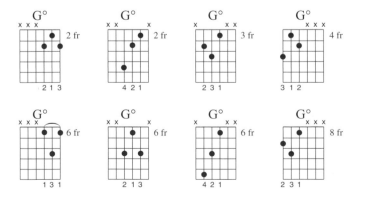

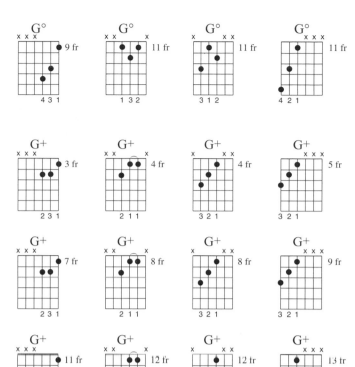

Augmented triads:

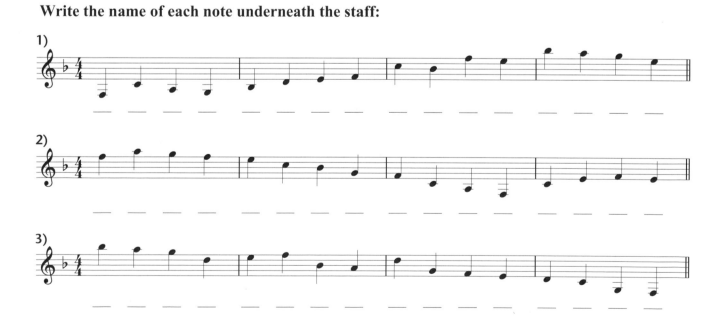

SIGHT-READING

Here are the notes of F major in second position.

Write the name of each note underneath the staff:

1)

2)

3)

Sight-Reading Exercise 15

F major, second position

Sight-Reading Exercise 16

F major, second position

SCALES AND TECHNIQUES

Three-Note-per-String Scales: Vertical Movement

The following examples come from the C major scale.

🔊 Track 23

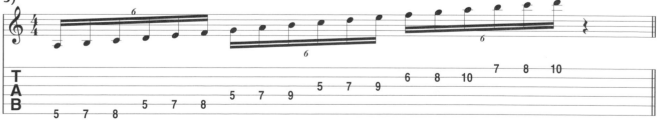

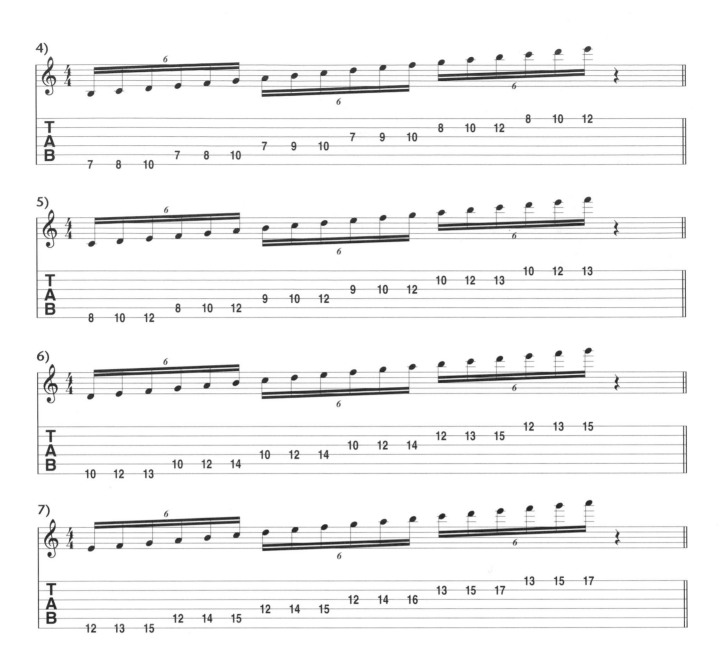

Three Note-per-String Scales: Horizontal Movement

Here we move horizontally through the patterns, two strings at a time.

Track 24

1st and 2nd strings:

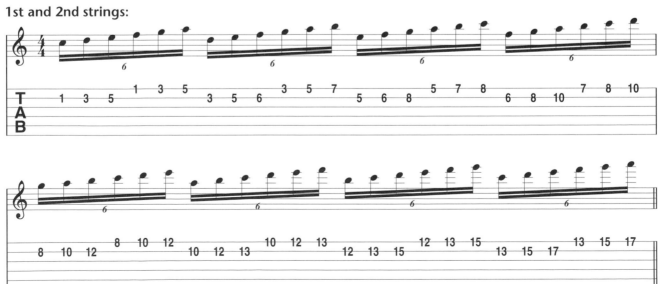

2nd and 3rd strings:

3rd and 4th strings:

4th and 5th strings:

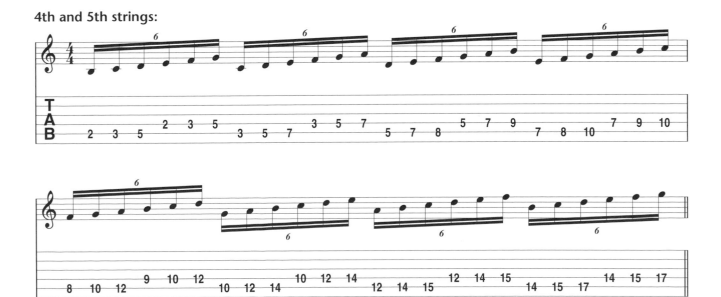

5th and 6th strings:

Three Note-per-String Scales: Variations

In these examples, we ascend vertically, horizontally, and diagonally up the neck.

Track 25

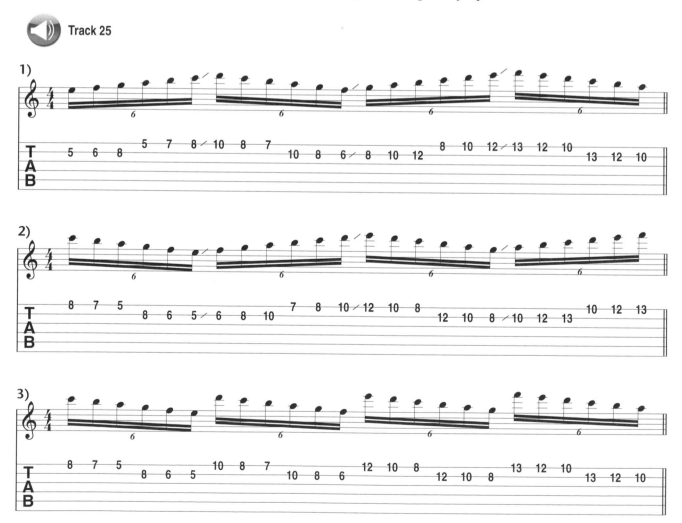

4)

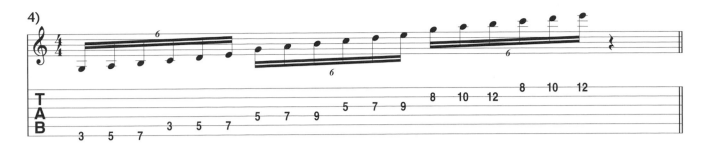

5)

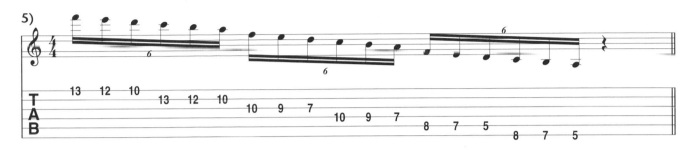

6)

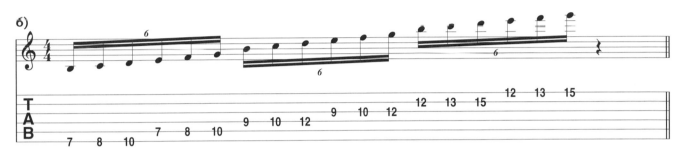

7)

etc.

LESSON 3

HARMONY AND THEORY

Triads: Review

Let's review what we've learned about triads so far:

1) They contain three different notes.

2) The qualities can be major (1–3–5), minor (1–♭3–5), diminished (1–♭3–♭5), or augmented (1–3–♯5).

3) They can be in root position (root on bottom), first inversion (3rd on bottom), or second inversion (5th on bottom).

4) A major scale harmonized in triads looks like this: I–ii–iii–IV–V–vi–vii°.

Naming Triads

You will probably see more than one way to name the same triad. I am going to show you the most common ones that you're likely to encounter. All names will apply to C triads and will appear in the order of most to least common.

> Major: C, Cmaj, Cma, or CM.
>
> Minor: Cm, Cmin, C–, or Cmi.
>
> Diminished: C° or Cdim.
>
> Augmented: C+ or Caug.

Inversions: To indicate that a triad is to be played in inversion, you can write the triad followed by a slash and a bass note. Here are some examples:

> C/E (C major in first inversion)
>
> C/G (C major in second inversion)
>
> Dm/A (D minor in second inversion)
>
> C+/E (C augmented in first inversion)
>
> B°/F (B diminished in second inversion)

RHYTHM CONCEPTS

Syncopation

The term *syncopation* refers to when a weaker beat or an upbeat is accented. When we count quarter notes in 4/4, normally the first and third beats are accented:

Sometimes, however, we'll hear the accented placed on weaker beats, creating a syncopation:

When we count eighth notes, beats 1, 2, 3, and 4 are called the *downbeats*; the "ands" in between them are called *upbeats*. Normally, the stress is placed on the downbeats.

When we place the stress on an upbeat, we again get syncopation:

Rhythm Exercise 17

Rhythm Exercise 18

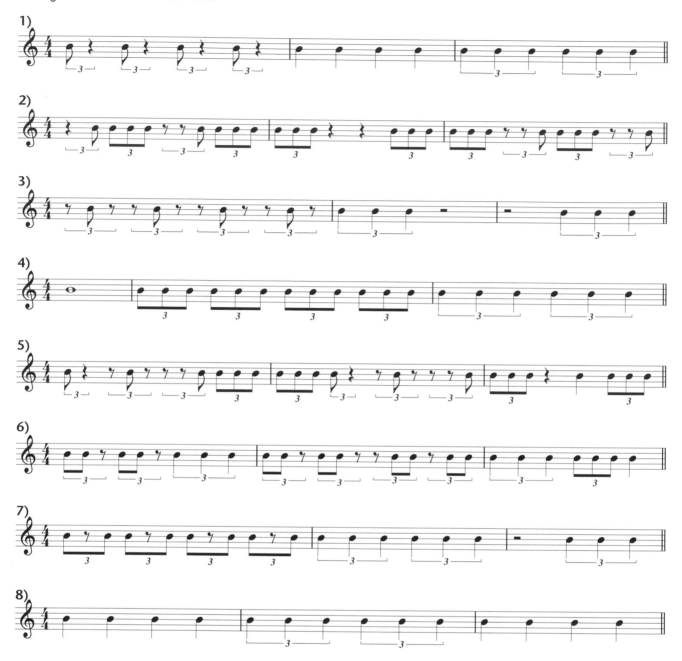

Four-Note Triad Voicings

When playing triads, it's very common to double the root note. The chord still only has three different notes, but it sounds a little more full because of the doubled root. Here we'll learn common voicings for our four different types of triads.

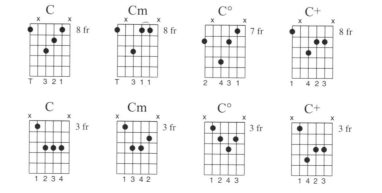

3) Root on 4th string

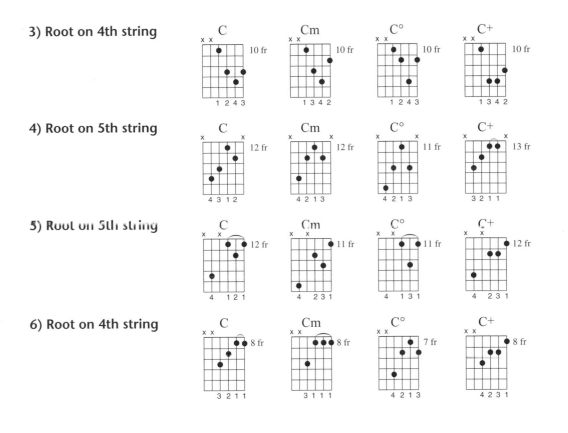

4) Root on 5th string

5) Root on 5th string

6) Root on 4th string

SIGHT-READING

Here are the notes of G major in second position.

Write the name of each note underneath the staff:

1)

2)

3)

Sight-Reading Exercise 17

G major, second position

Sight-Reading Exercise 18

G major, second position

SCALES AND TECHNIQUES

Major Triad Arpeggios

An *arpeggio* is simply the notes of a chord played in succession rather than simultaneously to form a melody. Here we're going to learn some common fingerings for major and minor triad arpeggios.

 Track 26

Diagonal movement

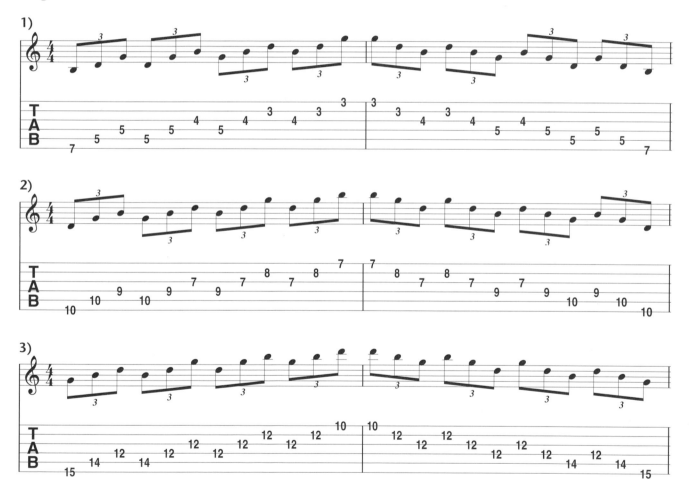

Horizonal movement

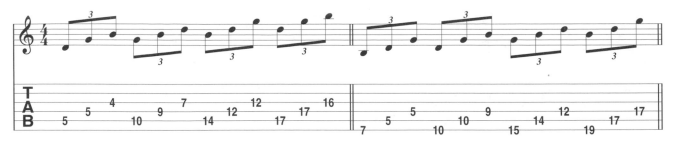

Vertical movement

5)

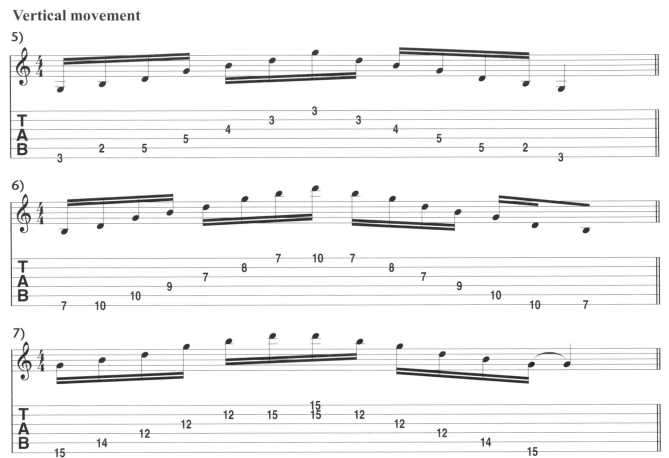

6)

7)

Minor Triad Arpeggios

 Track 27

Diagonal movement

1)

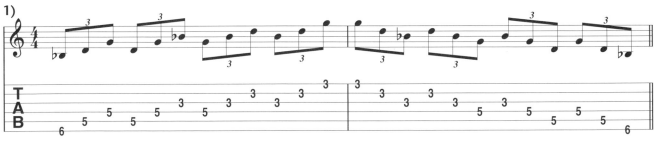

2)

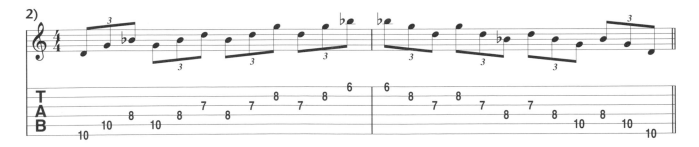

3)

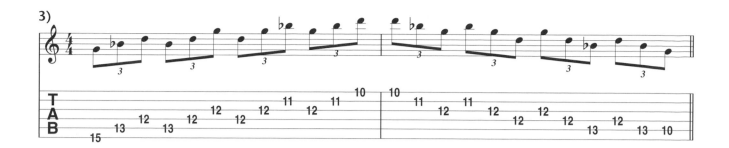

Horizonal movement

4)

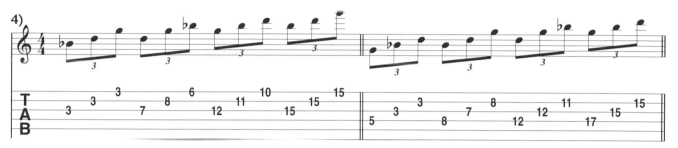

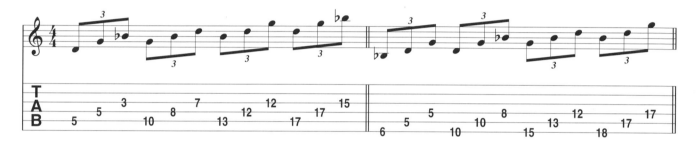

Vertical movement

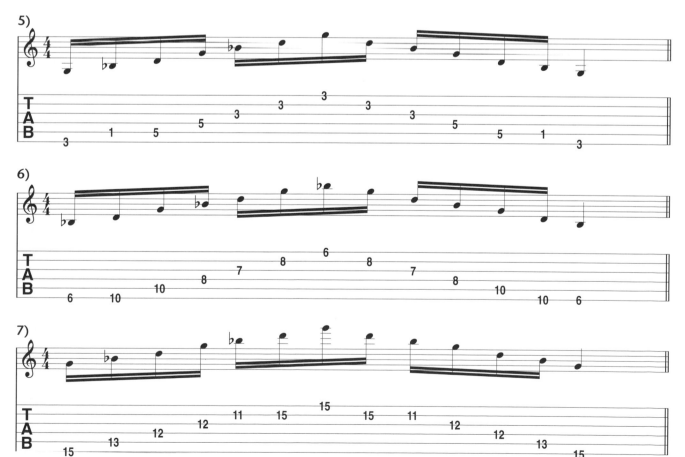

LESSON 4 • LATIN

BRAZILIAN RHYTHM PATTERNS

Latin music is very rhythmically driven, and different regions have traditional signature rhythmic patterns associated with them. Here we're going to learn some rhythmic patterns for two different Brazilian styles: the bossa nova and the samba. These examples are purely focused on rhythm, and therefore the notes you play are not important; you're just concentrating on the rhythms at this point. Try playing the down-stemmed notes with your thumb and the up-stemmed notes with your first or second finger.

Bossa Nova

The *bossa nova* is usually played at slow or medium tempos. Below we'll find a few common one- and two-measure patterns.

One-bar patterns:

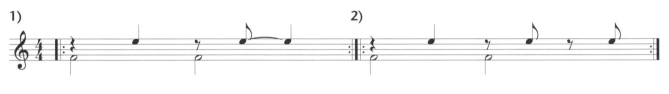

Two-bar patterns:

Samba

The *samba* is played at a faster tempo. Here are two different two-measure patterns. Notice that the patterns contain the same two measures; the order is just reversed.

AFRO-CUBAN RHYTHM PATTERNS

Now let's take a look at three common Afro-Cuban rhythms: the bolero, the cha cha, and mambo.

Bolero

The *bolero* is a slow rhythm. Watch for the triplet on the second half of beat 1.

Cha Cha

Here's a medium tempo pattern known as the *cha cha*. Be sure to count through the rests.

Mambo

The *mambo* is essentially a fast cha cha rhythm.

COMPING PATTERNS

Comping is a term used to describe the rhythm pattern (or patterns) you play beneath a lead instrument or vocalist. It is short for "accompanying." Here we're going to take some of our newly learned rhythms and put chords to them, thus creating several comping patterns.

Bossa Nova

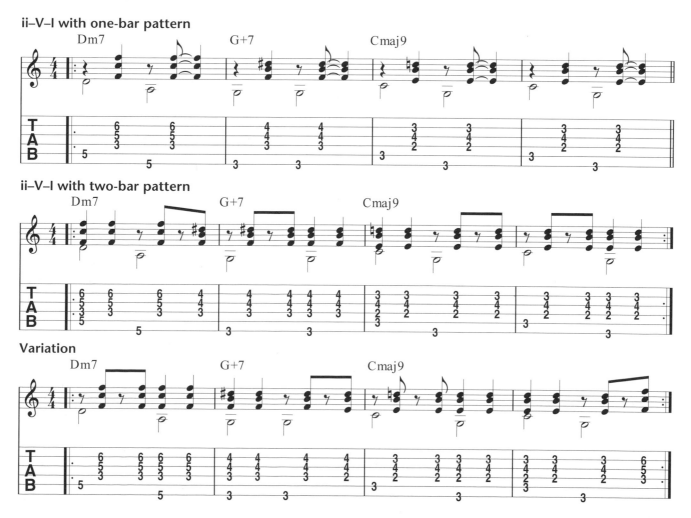

More variations

1a)

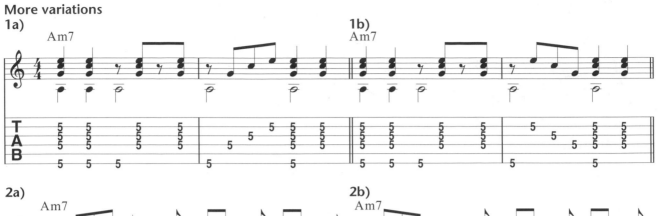

2a)

Bolero (slow)

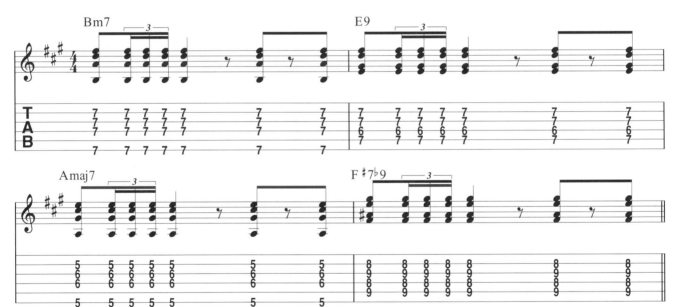

Cha Cha (medium)

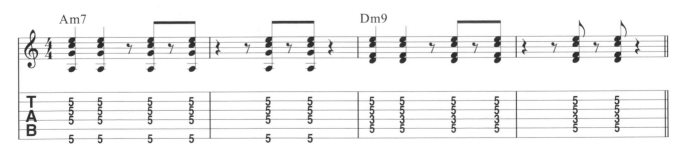

CHAPTER 4

LESSON 1

HARMONY AND THEORY

7th Chords

We have already learned that a triad is built by stacking two notes in 3rds above a root. A C major triad, for example, consists of the root, 3rd, and 5th of the major scale (C–E–G). If we continue this process of stacking 3rds with a fourth note, we end up with a 7th chord. Our C major triad, for example, would become a Cmaj7 chord if we remained in the C major scale. The notes would be the root, 3rd, 5th, and 7th of the major scale (C–E–G–B). If we were to build 7th chords off all the triads in the C major scale, it would look like this:

Let's take a look at the new intervals created by our additional note:

Cmaj7

- We have another major 3rd from G to B.
- We have a major 7th from C to B.
- The formula for a major 7th chord is 1–3–5–7.

Dm7

- We have another minor 3rd from A to C.
- We have a minor 7th from D to C.
- The formula for a minor 7th chord is 1–♭3–5–♭7.

Em7

- We have another minor 3rd from B to D.
- We have a minor 7th from E to D.

Fmaj7

- We have another major 3rd from C to E.
- We have a major 7th from F to E.

G7

- We have another minor 3rd from D to F.
- We have a minor 7th from G to F.
- The formula for a dominant 7th chord is 1–3–5–♭7.

Am7

- We have another minor 3rd from E to G.
- We have a minor 7th from A to G.

Bm7♭5

- We have another minor 3rd from F to A.
- We have a minor 7th from B to A.
- The formula for a minor 7♭5 chord is 1–♭3–♭5–♭7.

As you can see, we have four different types of 7th chords in the C major scale:

> Major 7th chords: Cmaj7 and Fmaj7
>
> Dominant 7th chords: G7
>
> Minor 7th chords: Dm7, Em7, and Am7
>
> Minor 7♭5 chords: Bmin7♭5

The Primary 7th Chords

We just learned how to construct the 7th chords from the major scale. This was accomplished by stacking a 3rd on top on the triad. This 3rd was either major or minor, depending on its place in the major scale. Now we're going to more fully explore 7th chord possibilities. We're going to stack first a major 3rd and then a minor 3rd on top of each of our four different triads (major, minor, diminished, and augmented) and see what we end up with.

Major Triad:

> If we stack a major 3rd on top, we get a major 7th chord: 1–3–5–7.
> If we stack a minor 3rd on top, we get a dominant 7th chord: 1–3–5–♭7.

Minor Triad:

> If we stack a major 3rd on top, we get a minor (major 7th) chord: 1–♭3–5–7.
> If we stack a minor 3rd on top, we get a minor 7th chord: 1–♭3–5–♭7.

Diminished Triad:

> If we stack a major 3rd on top, we get a minor 7♭5 chord: 1–♭3–♭5–♭7.
> If we stack a minor 3rd on top, we get a diminished 7th chord: 1–♭3–♭5–♭♭7.

Augmented Triad:

> If we stack a major 3rd on top, we'll end up with just an augmented triad again: 1–3–♯5–1.
> If we stack a minor 3rd on top, we get a major 7♯5 chord: 1–3–♯5–7.

This gives us a total of seven different 7th chords; these are our *primary 7th chords*. Below, we'll see how these seven chords look with a C root note:

RHYTHM CONCEPTS

Quarter-Note Triplets

Many players often have much more trouble learning to play quarter-note triplets than standard eighth-note triplets. This is perhaps because we are more used to hearing eighth-note triplets. Here I am going to show you an exercise to practice the quarter-note triplet.

First, play straight eighth-note triplets with alternate picking. You can practice this on any note you like:

Then mute all the upstrokes (every other note) with your left hand by releasing pressure off the fret:

After you have this down, don't connect on the upstrokes at all:

Now, if you replace the rest with another eighth note tied to the first one, you'll hear quarter-note triplets:

And that is exactly the same as this:

Rhythm Exercise 19

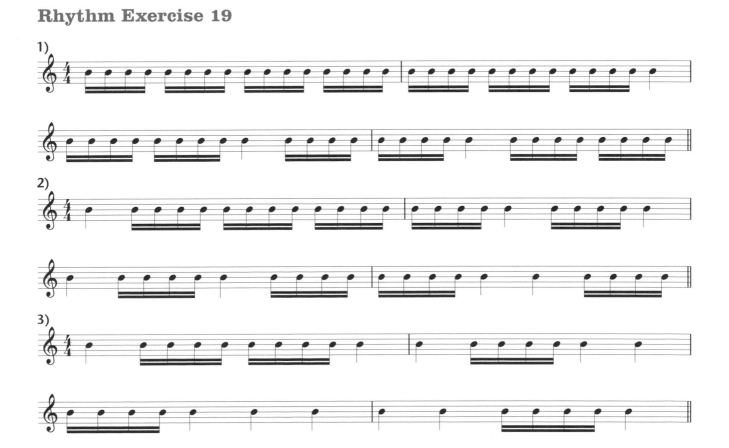

Rhythm Exercise 20

Sus4 Chords

When we play a triad built with a root, 4th, and 5th, we end up with a *sus4 chord* (1–4–5). "Sus" is short for "suspended," and it's named that because it sounds as though the 4th is "suspended" and needs to resolve to the 3rd. Below we'll see several voicings for sus4 chords:

1) Sus4 chords with open strings

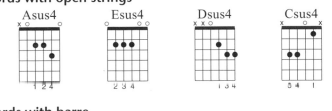

2) Sus4 chords with barre

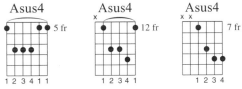

Sus2 Chords

In the same fashion that we san "suspend" the 4th in a triad, we can do the same with the 2nd. We end up with a *sus2 chord* (1–2–5). Below we'll find several voicings for sus2 chords:

1) Sus2 chords with open strings

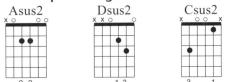

2) Sus2 chords with barre

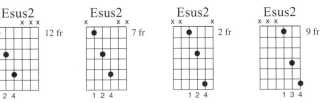

3) Stretch voicings

SIGHT-READING

Here we'll work on sight-reading in C major, fifth position. The circled notes can act as your new reference notes.

A B C D E F G A B C D E F G A B C

Write the name of each note underneath the staff:

Sight-Reading Exercise 19

C major, fifth position

Sight-Reading Exercise 20

C major, fifth position

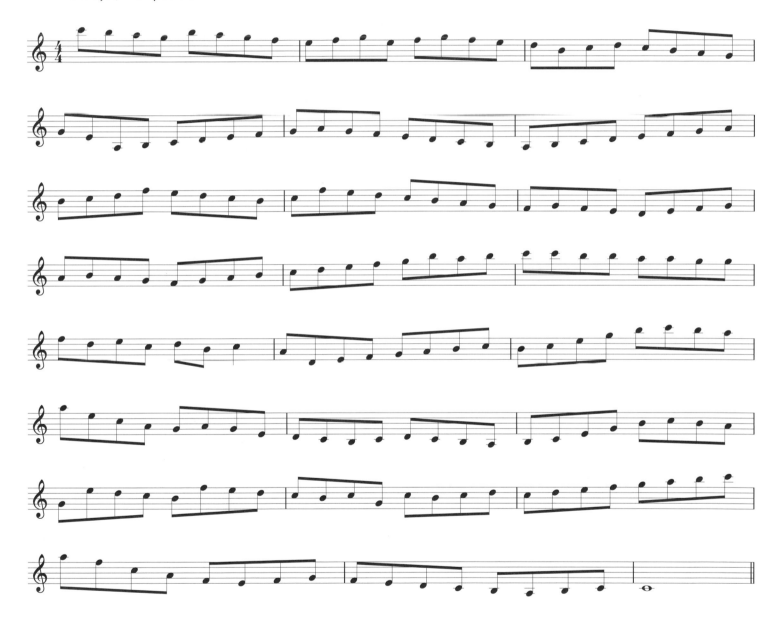

SCALES AND TECHNIQUES

7th Arpeggios

Here we'll learn the fingerings for four different types of 7th chord arpeggios: minor 7, dominant 7, major 7, and minor 7♭5. Each type will be presented in five patterns and one extended form.

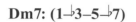 **Track 28**

Dm7: (1–♭3–5–♭7)

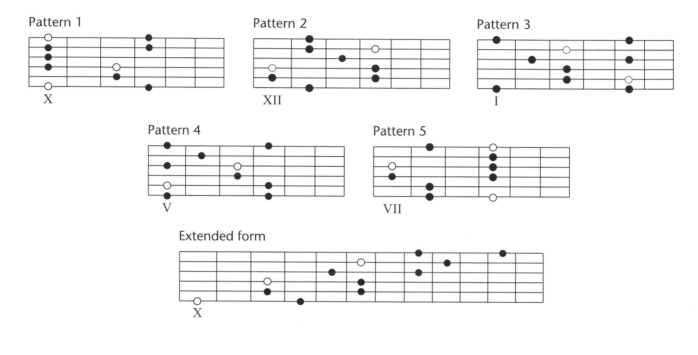

 Track 29

G7: (1–3–5–♭7)

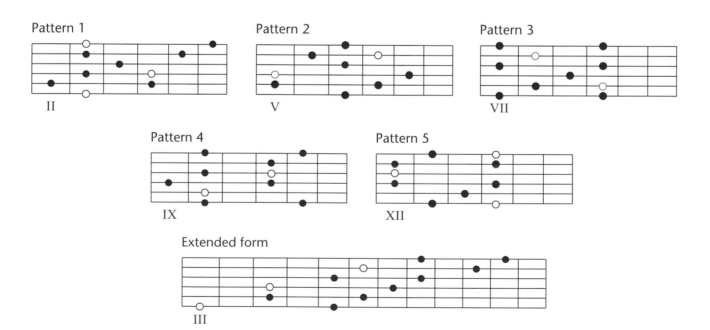

126

Cmaj7: (1–3–5–7)

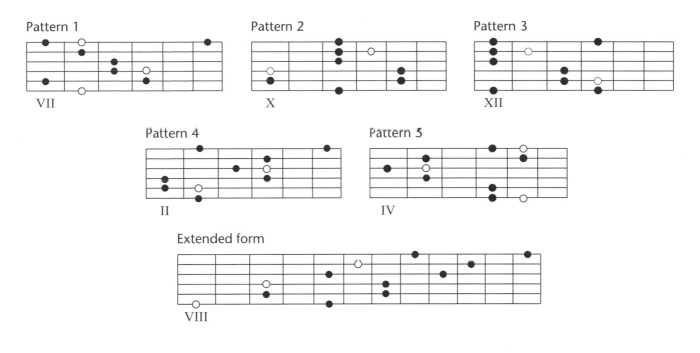

 Track 31

Bm7♭5: (1–♭3–♭5–♭7)

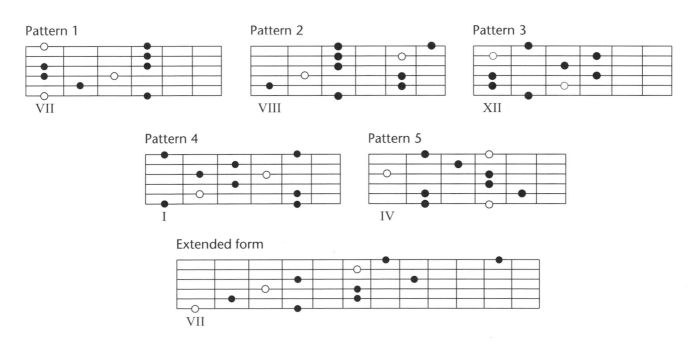

HARMONY AND THEORY

Extended Chords

If we continue the process of stacking 3rds onto our 7th chords, we get *extended chords*. There are three general types of extended chords: 9ths, 11ths, and 13ths. We're going to take a closer look at each in this section.

9th Chords

A *9th chord* results from stacking one 3rd on top of our 7th chord. We learned earlier that a Cmaj7 is spelled C–E–G–B (1–3–5–7). If we stack another 3rd on top of that, remaining in the C major scale, we end up with a Cmaj9 chord: C–E–G–B–D (1–3–5–7–9). If we were to build 9th chords off all the notes in the C major scale, it would look like this:

Let's take a look at the intervals of each:

Cmaj9 (C–E–G–B–D): 1–3–5–7–9

Dm9 (D–F–A–C–E): 1–♭3–5–♭7–9

Em7♭9 (E–G–B–D–F): 1–♭3–5–♭7–♭9

Fmaj9 (F–A–C–E–G): 1–3–5–7–9

G9 (G–B–D–F–A): 1–3–5–♭7–9

Am9 (A–C–E–G–B): 1–♭3–5–♭7–9

Bm7♭5♭9 (B–D–F–A–C): 1–♭3–♭5–♭7–♭9

11th Chords

If we continue the process and stack another third on the top of the 9th chord, we get *11th chords*. Below we'll find all the 11th chords of the C major scale:

Let's take a look at the intervals of each:

Cmaj11 (C–E–G–B–D–F): 1–3–5–7–9–11

Dm11 (D–F–A–C–E–G): 1–♭3–5–♭7–9–11

Em11♭9 (E–G–B–D–F–A): 1–♭3–5–♭7–♭9–11

Fmaj7♯11 (F–A–C–E–G–B): 1–3–5–7–9–♯11

G11 (G–B–D–F–A–C): 1–3–5–♭7–9–11

Am11 (A–C–E–G–B–D): 1–♭3–5–♭7–9–11

Bm11♭9♭5 (B–D–F–A–C–E): 1–♭3–♭5–♭7–♭9–11

13th Chords

If we stack another 3rd on the top of the 11th chords, we get *13th chords*. This is as extended as we can get! Below we'll find the 13th chords of the C major scale:

Cmaj13 (C–E–G–B–D–F–A): 1–3–5–7–9–11–13

Dm13 (D–F–A–C–E–G–B): 1–♭3–5–♭7–9–11–13

Em7♭13♭9 (E–G–B–D–F–A–C): 1–♭3–5–♭7–♭9–11–♭13

Fmaj13♯11 (F–A–C–E–G–B–D): 1–3–5–7–9–♯11–13

G13 (G–B–D–F–A–C–E): 1–3–5–♭7–9–11–13

Am7♭13 (A–C–E–G–B–D–F): 1–♭3–5–♭7–9–11–♭13

Bm7♭5♭9♭13 (B–D–F–A–C–E–G): 1–♭3–♭5–♭7–♭9–11–♭13

It should be noted that, in extended chords, it is not necessary (and in fact it is unusual) for all of the notes to be present. Generally speaking, the root, 3rd, 7th, and the highest extension are usually present. The 5th and lower extensions are sometimes left out. For example, in a Dm11 chord, the 5th (A) and 9th (E) may or may not be present, but the root (D), ♭3rd (F), ♭7th (C), and 11th (G) would be present. In a G13 chord, the 5th (D), 9th (A) and 11th (C) may or may not be present, but the root (G), 3rd (B), ♭7th (F), and 13th (E) would be present.

RHYTHM CONCEPTS

Half-Note Triplets

Half-note triplets are usually even more difficult to play than quarter-note triplets. But we can again use an exercise to learn how to hear them. Let's look first again at eighth-note triplets:

Now, split the whole measure into groups of four notes. Play the first note of each group and mute the following three triplets. You'll notice that all three notes that you play unmuted are all downstrokes.

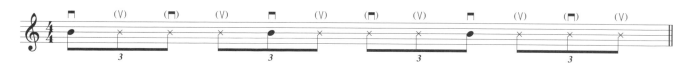

The next step is to replace the muted notes with rests:

Now, sustain those three notes instead of leaving rests between them. You should still go through the picking motion as if you were playing. It helps to think of a triplet tied to three more triplets. It looks like this:

You've just played half-note triplets!

Rhythm Exercise 21

Rhythm Exercise 22

Funk Chords

Here we'll take a look at some of the common voicings that are used in funk guitar. Typically, full six-string chords are not used, as they tend to sound a little too cumbersome for the often-syncopated rhythms of funk. Four-note voicings are much more common, as are triads and dyads. Here we'll learn several typical four-note chords used in funk styles:

1) Triads

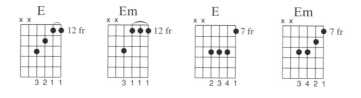

2) 7th chords

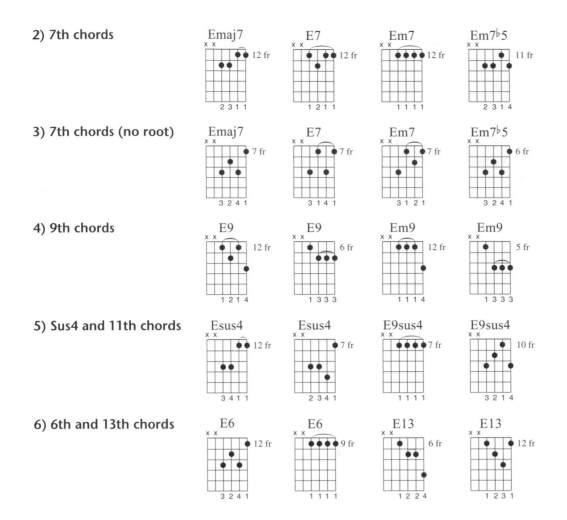

3) 7th chords (no root)

4) 9th chords

5) Sus4 and 11th chords

6) 6th and 13th chords

SIGHT-READING

Here we see the notes of F major in fifth position. The circled notes are still your reference notes.

A B♭ C D E F G A B♭ C D E F G A B♭ C

Write the name of each note underneath the staff:

1)

2)

3)

SIGHT-READING EXERCISE 21

F major, fifth position

SIGHT-READING EXERCISE 22

F major, fifth position

SCALES AND TECHNIQUES

Practicing Arpeggios

In the following examples, I am going to show you several ways to practice arpeggios. These examples will be for an Am7 arpeggio. Be sure to practice all different types of arpeggios and transpose them to different keys.

 Track 32

1)

2) Groups of 3: (1–♭3–5, ♭3–5–♭7, 5–♭7–1, ♭7–1–♭3)

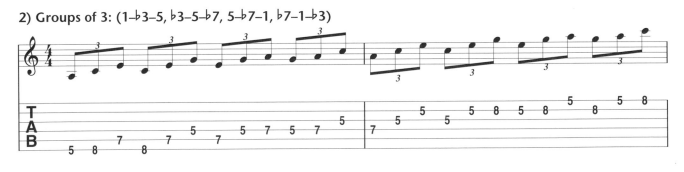

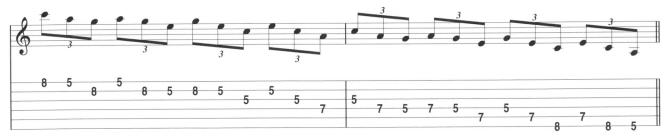

134

3) Groups of 4: (1–♭3–5–♭7, ♭3–5–♭7–1, 5–♭7–1–♭3, ♭7–1–♭3–5)

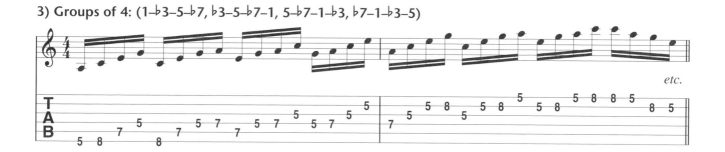

etc.

4) Groups of 4, reversed: (♭7–5–♭3–1, 1–♭7–5–♭3, ♭3–1–♭7–5, 5–♭3–1–♭7)

5) Groups of 3, reversed: (5–♭3–1, ♭7–5–♭3, 1–♭7–5, ♭3–1–♭7)

etc.

6) Arpeggios with skips: (1–5–♭3–♭7–5–1–♭7–♭3)

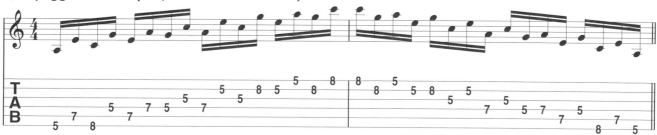

HARMONY AND THEORY

The Function of Chords

We have three major triads and three minor triads in the major scale. As you'll remember, the major triads are I, IV, and V, while the minor triads are ii, iii, and vi. The major triads are known as the *primary triads,* and the minor triads are known as the *secondary triads.*

Each of these triads has another name as well. We refer to the I triad as the *tonic.* The IV is known as the *subdominant.* And the V is known as the *dominant.*

The secondary triads are all related in 3rds to the primary triads. If you go down a minor 3rd from the tonic, you have the vi. If you go down a minor 3rd from the subdominant, you have the ii. If you go down a minor 3rd from the dominant, you have the iii. These triads also have other names. The iv is the *tonic parallel,* the ii is the *subdominant parallel,* and the iii is the *dominant parallel.*

As you can see, both groups of triads exist in a I–IV–V relationship:

| I | IV | V | vi | ii | iii |

The Cadence

A *cadence* is a sequence of chords connected in a musical way that resolves to a final chord. There are several different types of cadences. Here are some of the most common:

V–I: This is known as a *perfect cadence.* This is the most final cadence that you can have; many phrases or entire songs end with this type of cadence.

IV–I: This is known as a *plagal cadence.* This cadence doesn't provide the finality of the perfect cadence. It reaches the I chord a little more gently. This is also nicknamed the *amen cadence* because of its use in many church hymns.

We can also have what's known as an *imperfect cadence.* This type of cadence exists when a sequence of chords leads to a V chord instead of the I chord. Some examples of this would be: I–V, I–IV–V.

RHYTHM CONCEPTS

Triplet Combinations

Below we'll find several different combinations of triplets. In examples 2–7, measure 1 notates the best method for counting measure 2.

1) Eighth notes

2) Quarter notes

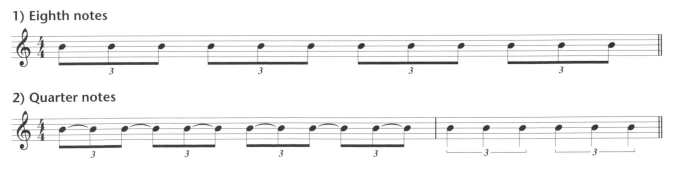

3) Half note/quarter note

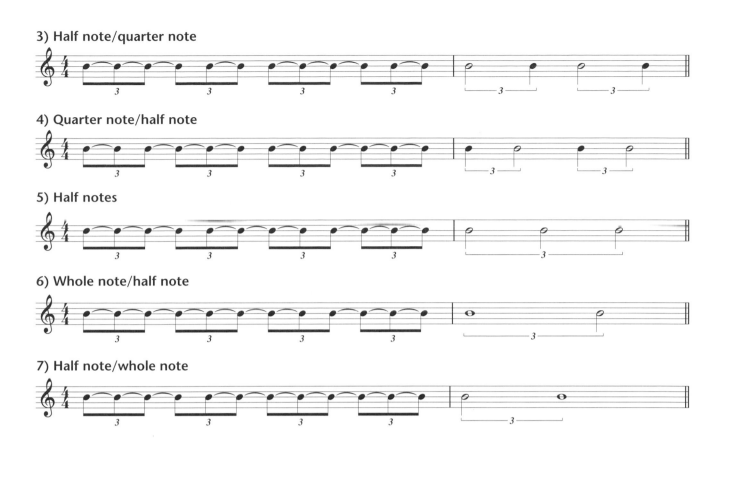

4) Quarter note/half note

5) Half notes

6) Whole note/half note

7) Half note/whole note

Rhythm Exercise 23

1)

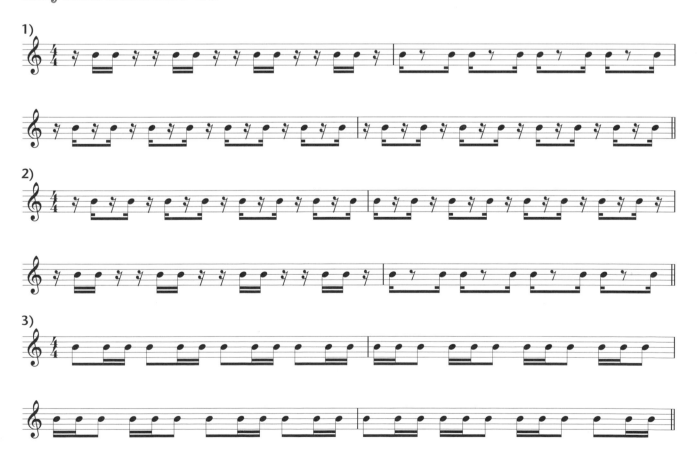

2)

3)

Rhythm Exercise 24

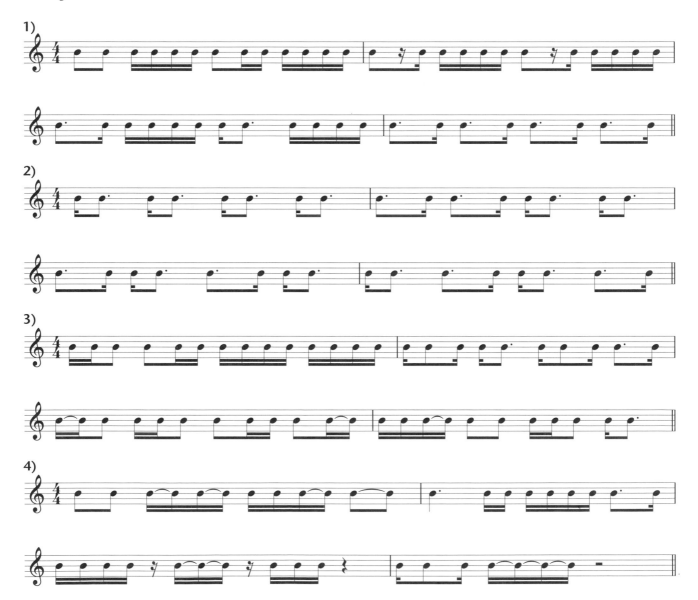

Harmonized C Major Scale

Here we'll learn voicings to play through all of the chords of a C major scale in triads and 7th chords. The triads are presented in root position, first inversion, and second inversion. The 7th chords are presented with roots on the sixth, fifth, and fourth strings.

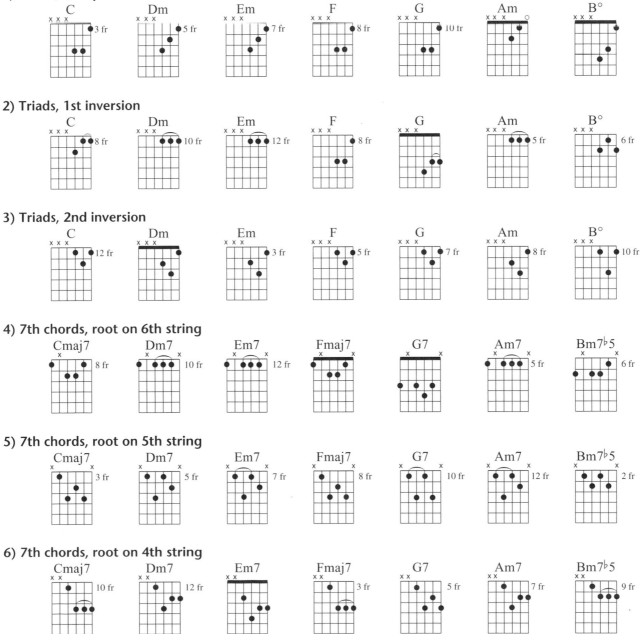

SIGHT-READING

Here we see the notes of G major in fifth position. The circled notes are still your reference notes.

G A B C D E F# G A B C D E F# G A B C

Write the name of each note underneath the staff:

Sight-Reading Exercise 23

G major, fifth position

Sight-Reading Exercise 24

G major, fifth position

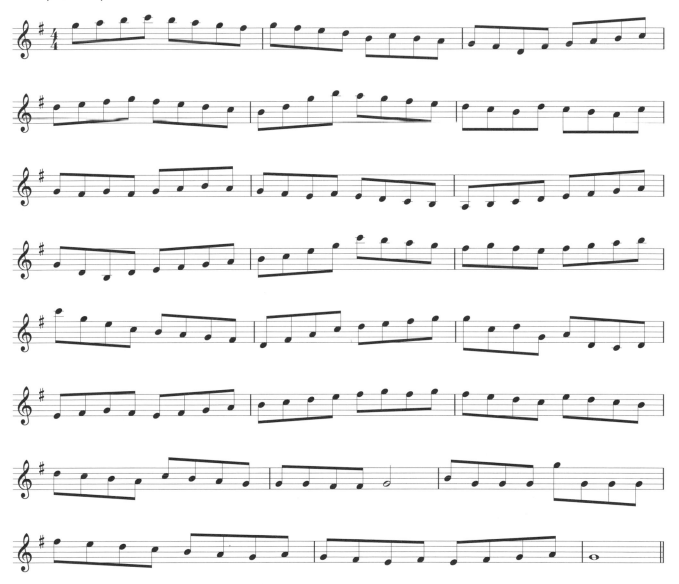

SCALES AND TECHNIQUES

Rhythmic Displacement

Rhythmic displacement is an easy way to make improvising more interesting. The technique basically involves playing a numbered sequence of notes in a different rhythm, so that the first note of each sequence will not fall directly on a beat each time. For example, instead of playing a four-note sequence in sixteenth notes, you can play the same sequence in a triplet rhythm. This will displace the sequence rhythmically and make it very interesting to listen to.

Here we see this technique applied to the A minor pentatonic scale:

Track 33

1a) Groups of 4, sixteenth notes

1b) Groups of 4, triplets

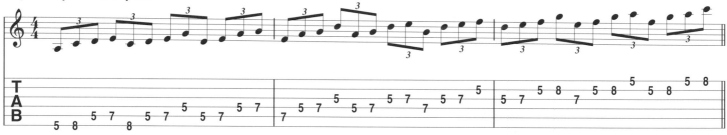

2a) Groups of 3, triplets

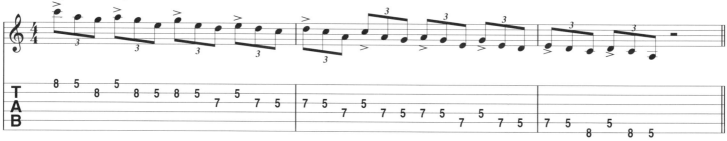

2b) Groups of 3, sixteenth notes

And now the same technique is shown with the three-note-per-string C major scale:

3a) Group of 6, sixteenth-note triplets

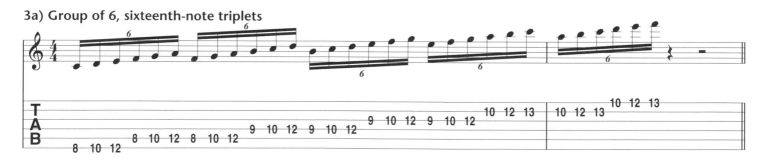

3b) Group of 6, sixteenth notes

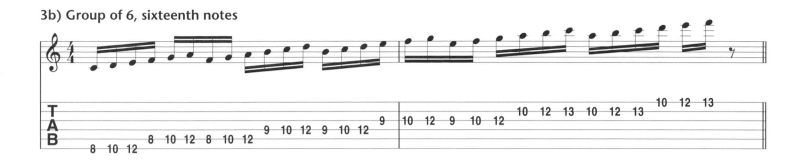

LESSON 4 • FUNK

SYNCOPATION EXERCISES

In order to master funk guitar, you must master the art of syncopated rhythms. Sixteenth-note syncopations are very common in funk, and the exercises below are designed to help you become familiar with this concept. Choose any note you like. For the muted notes, just slightly release the pressure so that a deadened sound is produced. This sound is integral to the funk style.

Sixteenth notes

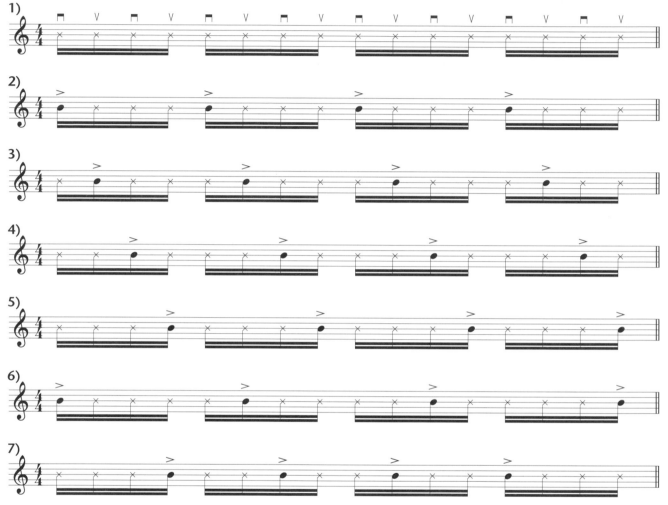

Typical Sixteenth-Note Rhythms

Now let's take a look at some of the various sixteenth-note rhythms you'll come across in this style. For these examples, you can either play a ghost stroke for the rest (not contact the string at all) or play a dead note. Make sure your right hand is continually moving in sixteenth notes to keep the rhythm. The accents of the notes should come from your left hand.

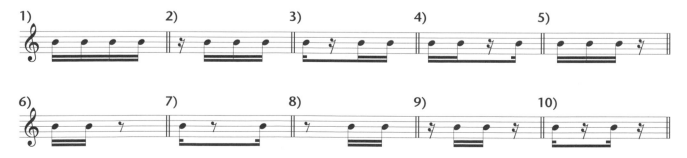

TRIPLETS

There are two different types of strumming for triplets: straight alternate picking, and alternate picking starting with a downstroke on each downbeat. The latter of these two methods is normally used for slower to medium tempos.

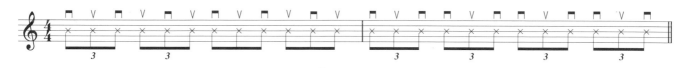

Use alternate picking for all of the rhythm exercises.

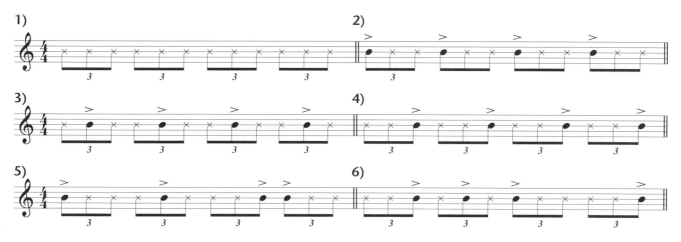

Typical Triplet Rhythms

Here we see some of the syncopated triplet rhythms you'll come across in funk. Remember to keep your right hand moving and practice these with both rests and dead notes.

FUNK GROOVES

Here we'll see these techniques applied to some typical funk grooves. If you haven't been, you should definitely be practicing these with a metronome! Rhythm is everything in funk. If you're not "in the pocket," it's not going to groove.

One-Chord Grooves

Here we see a Bm7 chord treated to several different rhythms. Remember to keep your right hand moving.

1)

2)

3)

4)

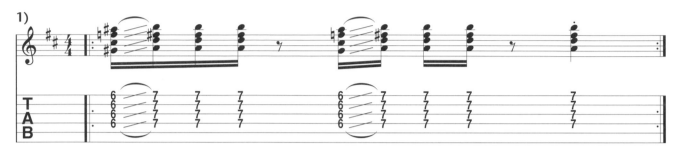

Single-Note Grooves

These grooves feature mostly riffing, single-note work. Try practicing these with a slight palm mute as well.

Octave Grooves

Octaves are used much in the same way as single notes. Below you'll find an octave fingering for the A minor pentatonic scale followed by a two-measure riff. Remember to mute all the strings you're not playing so you don't get any extraneous notes or open strings.

Triplet Grooves

Experiment with the two different types of picking over these triplet grooves. You may find that one suits your style better.

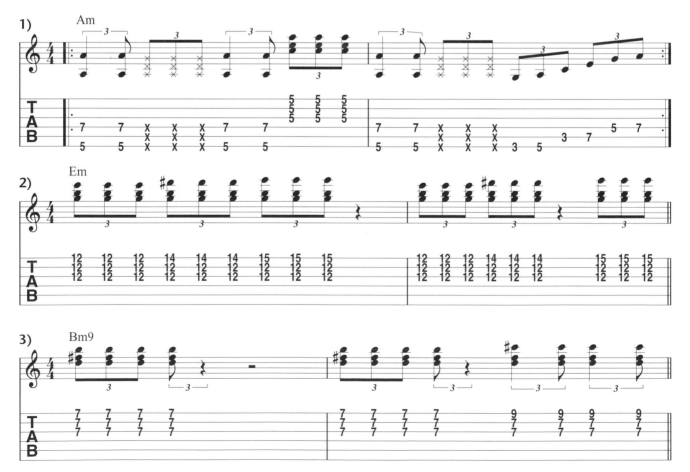

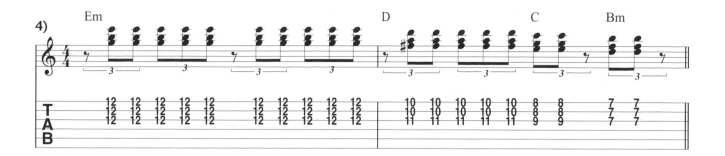

IMPROVISING CONCEPTS

Rhythmic Motives

Many times in funk, you can get by just fine by using the minor pentatonic scale. Again, rhythm is almost more important here than the notes you play. The concept of *rhythmic motives* can strengthen your feel and provide coherence to your solo. On the first staff below, we see a rhythmic motive. This same motive will be used to generate several different phrases that follow.

Rhythmic motive:

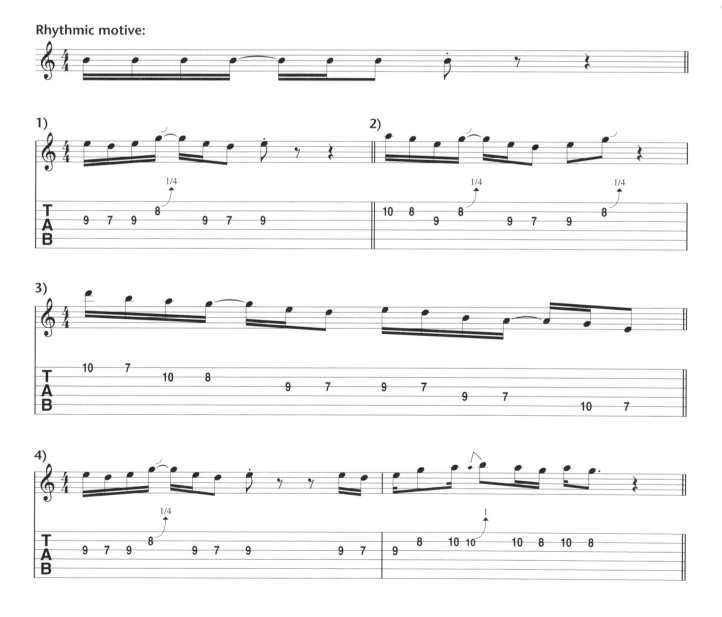

HARMONY AND THEORY

The Modes of the Major Scale

We touched briefly on the subject of modes earlier. In this section, we're going to more fully explore them. We know that the major scale consists of seven different modes—one for each note of the scale. Below we'll review the modes in C major. Notice the chord symbols that tell the nature of the mode and its extensions.

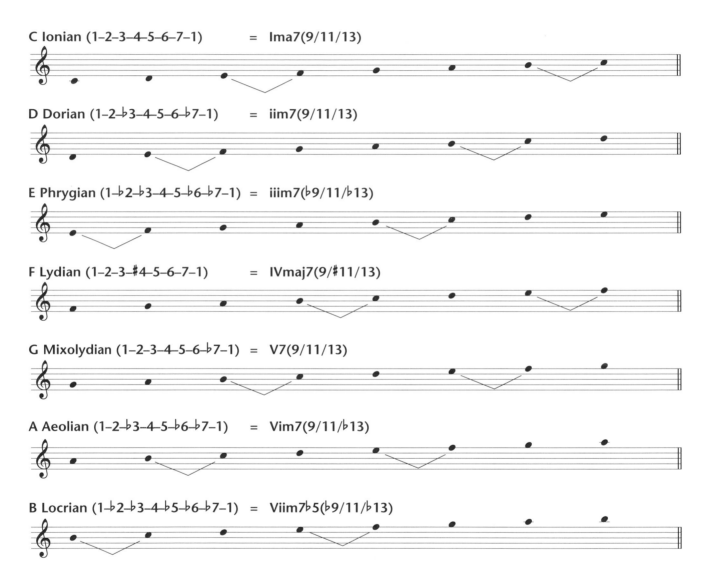

C Ionian (1–2–3–4–5–6–7–1) = Ima7(9/11/13)

D Dorian (1–2–♭3–4–5–6–♭7–1) = iim7(9/11/13)

E Phrygian (1–♭2–♭3–4–5–♭6–♭7–1) = iiim7(♭9/11/♭13)

F Lydian (1–2–3–♯4–5–6–7–1) = IVmaj7(9/♯11/13)

G Mixolydian (1–2–3–4–5–6–♭7–1) = V7(9/11/13)

A Aeolian (1–2–♭3–4–5–♭6–♭7–1) = Vim7(9/11/♭13)

B Locrian (1–♭2–♭3–4–♭5–♭6–♭7–1) = Viim7♭5(♭9/11/♭13)

You can divide the modes very roughly into major and minor modes. The modes with major 7th and dominant 7th tonalities belong to the major modes. The modes with minor 7th and minor 7♭5 tonalities belong to the minor modes.

Major modes:	**Minor modes:**
Ionian	Dorian
Lydian	Aeolian
Mixolydian	Phrygian

The Locrian mode is a special case because the minor 7♭5 chord is not stable enough to function as a tonic chord. It is good to be able to hear the difference between the different modes. Each has its own characteristic sound. Below we see the defining elements of each mode's sound:

Ionian: Major 7th with a natural 4

Dorian: Minor 7th with a natural 6

Phrygian: Minor 7th with a ♭2

Lydian: Major 7th with a ♯4

Mixolydian: Dominant 7th

Aeolian: Minor 7th with a ♭6

Locrian: Minor 7♭5 with a ♭2

Here we see the closed-position fingerings for the modes of C major:

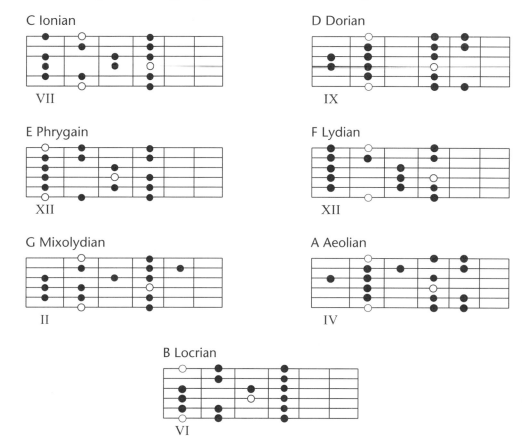

RHYTHM CONCEPTS

Shuffle Feel

A *shuffle feel* is popular in many blues and rock tunes. What constitutes a shuffle is a triplet undercurrent throughout the song. The eighth notes are not played as standard eighth notes. Rather, they are played as a triplets with the first two tied together. See below:

Many times, you'll see a shuffle written with standard eighth notes. An indication at the beginning of the piece will tell you that the eighth notes are to be played with a shuffle feel.

Rhythm Exercise 25

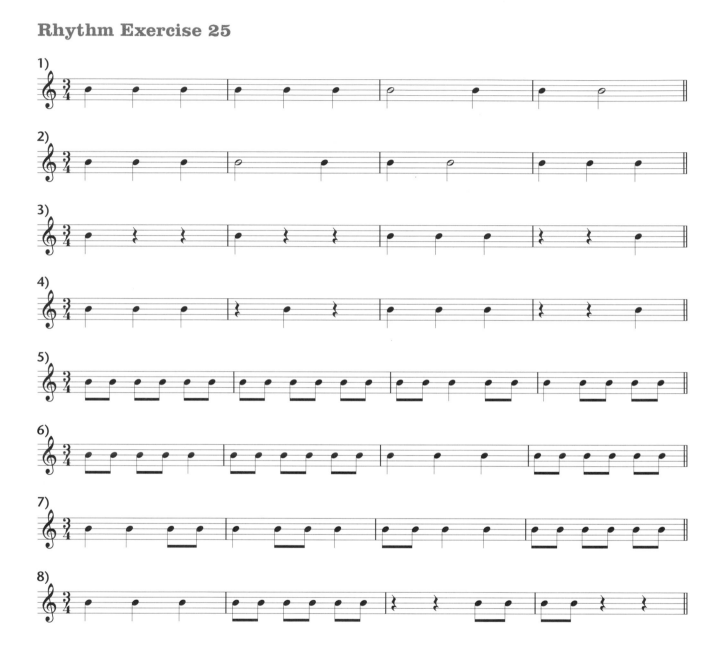

Rhythm Exercise 26

9th Chords

Here we see several different voicings for different types of 9th chords.

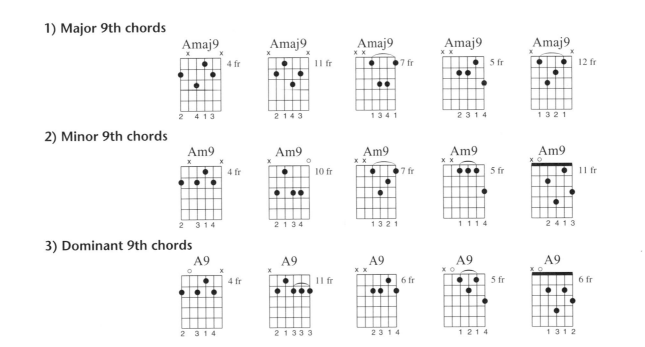

1) Major 9th chords

2) Minor 9th chords

3) Dominant 9th chords

13th Chords

Here we see voicings for a few different 13th chords.

1) Major 13th and dominant 13th chords

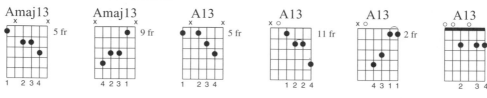

2) Minor 13th chords

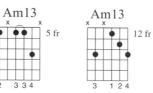

SIGHT-READING

It's just as important to be able to read chord charts as it is to read single notes. Here's a few exercises:

Chord Chart Reading Exercise 1

Chord Chart Reading Exercise 2

SCALES AND TECHNIQUES

Legato Playing

To play *legato* means to play everything very smoothly, letting each note sound as long as possible. This can create a feel of "flowing" through the lines. Instead of picking every single note, you pick only when you change strings. Use hammer-ons and pull-offs to connect the notes on the same string (also referred to as *slurs*). Try to maintain the same volume between the picked notes and the legato notes. Play the following examples on each string:

Track 34

Repeating Scalar Patterns

Here are several different repeating patterns for you to practice. They require quite a bit of stamina and really give your fingers a workout. Examples 1–12 are in A minor, while examples 13–16 are in E minor pentatonic.

Track 35

Pentatonic Sequences

The following examples are derived from the A minor pentatonic scale in root position. Remember to try and maintain consistent volume. Note that example 5 is based on A minor and contains notes outside of the pentatonic scale.

 Track 36

Major Scales: Diagonal Movement

Here we see the notes of C major arranged in a four-note-per-string diagonal pattern. You'll pick only the first note on each string, hammer on (or pull off) the second and third notes, and slide up (or down) to the fourth note.

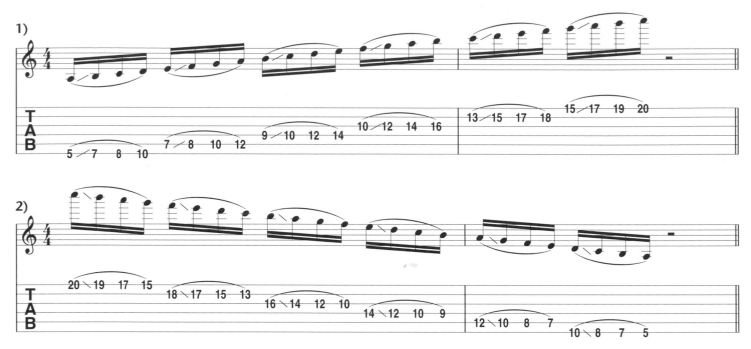

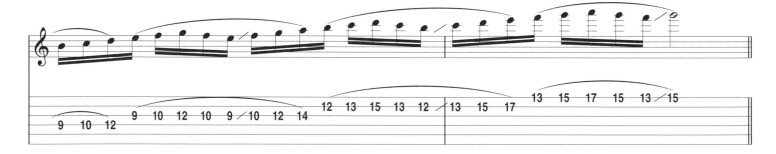

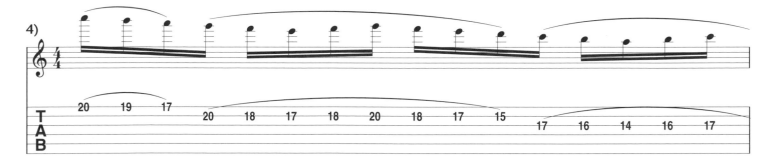

Major Scales: Horizontal Movement

In these examples, we work mostly on one string and cover the whole neck. Try playing these examples on each string.

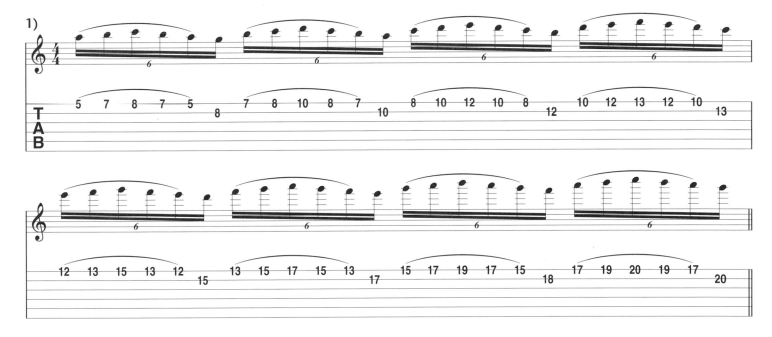

Track 37

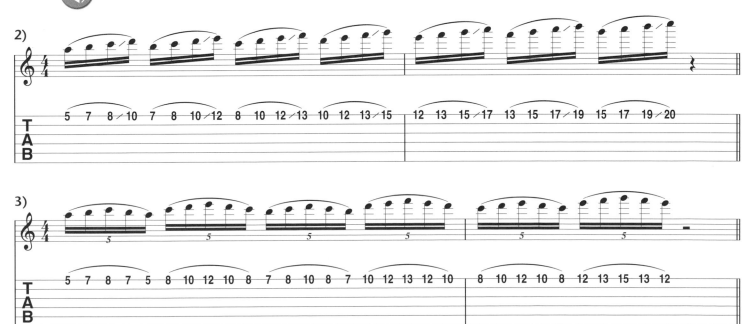

LESSON 2

HARMONY AND THEORY

The Modes of the Major Scale II

Previously, we learned how to construct and play the modes in C major. This wasn't too difficult, as we were really just playing the C major scale starting from a different note each time. Now, however, we're going to play all seven modes with A as the root. So, each one is going to be in a different key, and it will require you to really know your modes. Here are the forms:

A Ionian: A–B–C♯–D–E–F♯–G♯–A

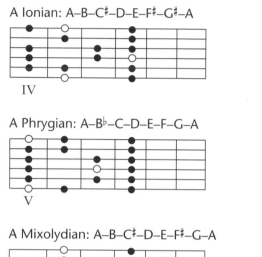

A Dorian: A–B–C–D–E–F♯–G–A

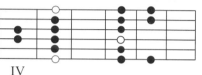

A Phrygian: A–B♭–C–D–E–F–G–A

A Lydian: A–B–C♯–D♯–E–F♯–G♯–A

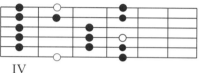

A Mixolydian: A–B–C♯–D–E–F♯–G–A

A Aeolian: A–B–C–D–E–F–G–A

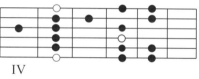

A Locrian: A–B♭–C–D–E♭–F–G–A

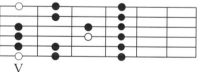

Below, we'll see which key each of the above modes comes from:

A Ionian = A major (A–B–C♯–D–E–F♯–G♯)

A Dorian = G major (G–A–B–C–D–E–F♯)

A Phrygian = F major (F–G–A–B♭–C–D–E)

A Lydian = E major (E–F♯–G♯–A–B–C♯–D♯)

A Mixolydian = D major (D–E–F♯–G–A–B–C♯)

A Aeolian = C major (C–D–E–F–G–A–B)

A Locrian = B♭ major (B♭–C–D–E♭–F–G–A)

RHYTHM CONCEPTS

Odd Groupings

Outside of triplets, you'll see a few other note groupings that aren't evenly divided. These are known as *odd groupings*. They can consist of basically any number, but the most popular are quintuplets (groups of five), septuplets (groups of seven), and ninetuplets (groups of nine). See below for examples of these:

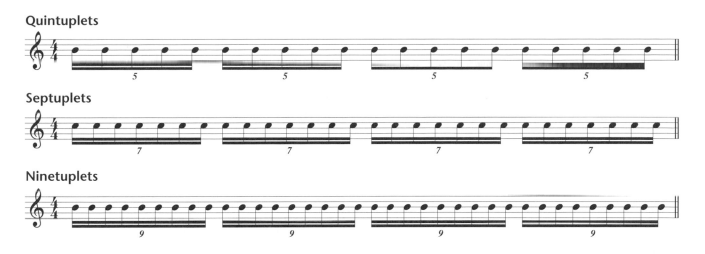

Here we see these groupings applied in different licks. Example 3 is the same group of five from example 1, but they're played in straight sixteenth notes. This creates a rhythmic displacement that we talked about earlier. Example 5 is related to example 4 the same way.

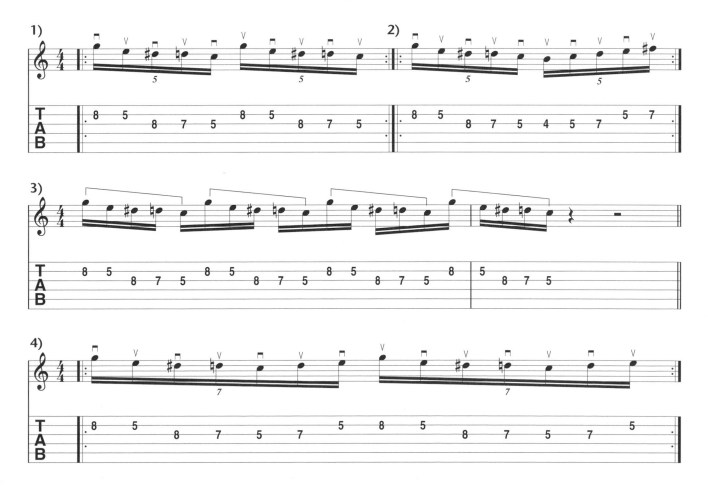

One of the problems that odd groupings create deals with picking. Since they are uneven-numbered groupings, alternate picking is sometimes difficult. An alternative to this is called *economy picking*. It involves using the same pick direction whenever possible while crossing strings. The examples below demonstrate this:

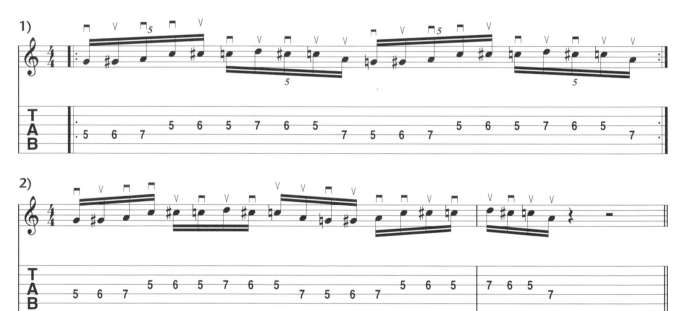

Rhythm Exercise 27

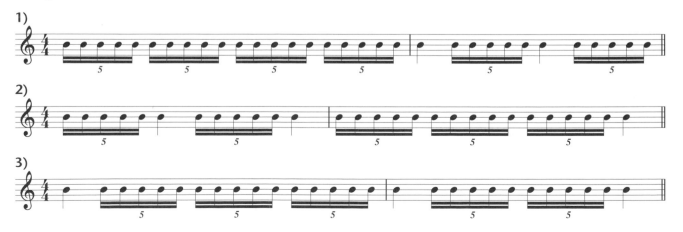

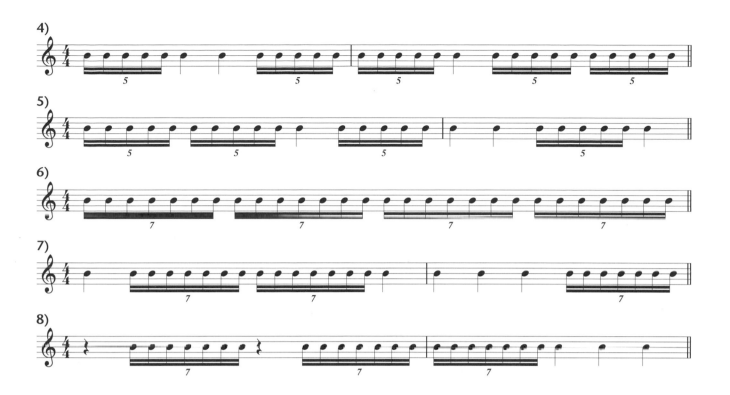

Rhythm Exercise 28

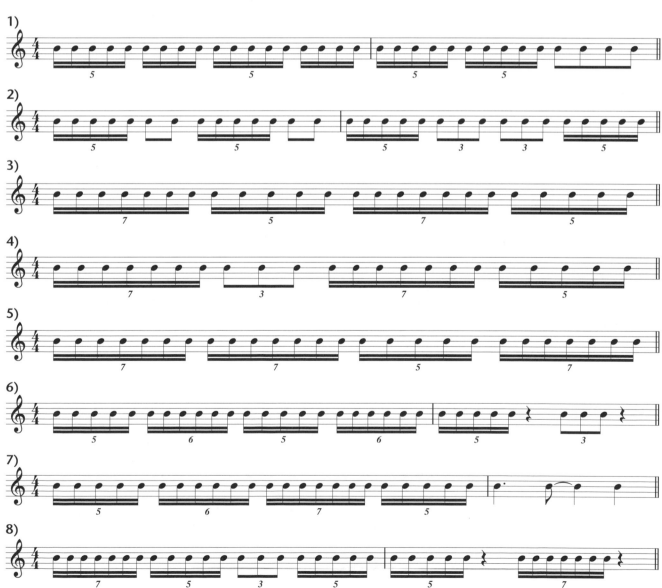

11th Chords

Here we see some voicings for different types of 11th chords:

1) Major 7♯11 chords

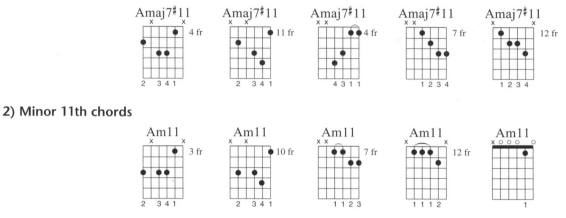

2) Minor 11th chords

Dominant Sus Chords

Here we see voicings for Dominant 7sus4 chords and Dominant 7sus9 chords:

1) Dominant 7sus4 chords

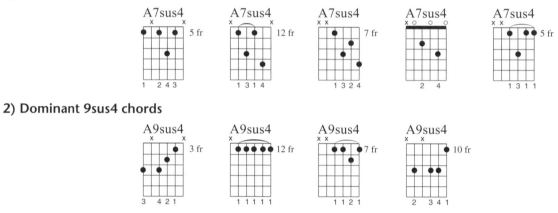

2) Dominant 9sus4 chords

Altered Chords

An *altered* chord exists when one or more of the extensions (9, 11, 13) have been raised or lowered by a half step. These are most common in jazz, as they usually increase the amount of tension the chord produces. Below we'll see several examples of altered chords:

1) Dominant 7♭13 chords

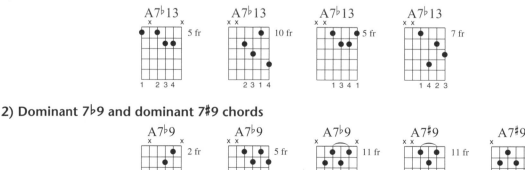

2) Dominant 7♭9 and dominant 7♯9 chords

3) Dominant 7#11 chords

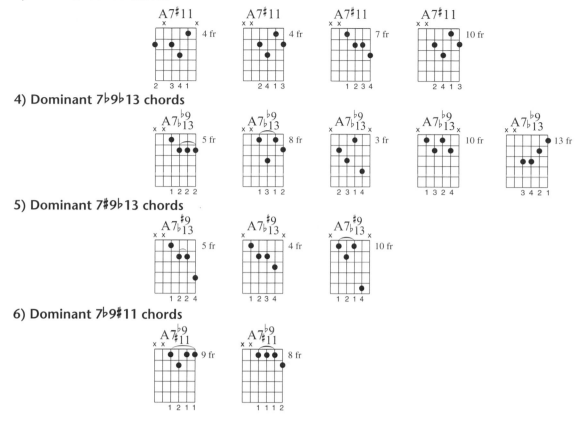

4) Dominant 7♭9♭13 chords

5) Dominant 7#9♭13 chords

6) Dominant 7♭9#11 chords

SIGHT-READING

Use barre chords for the following two exercises.

Chord Chart Reading Exercise 3

Chord Chart Reading Exercise 4

SCALES AND TECHNIQUES: TAPPING

Tapping is a technique that incorporates your right hand on the fretboard. It is essentially the same thing as performing a hammer-on and pull-off with a finger on your right hand. You can either use your index finger, meaning you have to find a place for your pick, or you can use your middle finger, which allows you to keep the pick in your hand. After tapping the note, you can pull it off downwards or upwards, depending on your preference.

Tapping Triad Arpeggios

Probably the most common type of tapping is triad arpeggio licks. This type of playing was popularized by Eddie Van Halen in the eighties. Here we see several examples, and a sequence that follows a chord progression.

🔊 **Track 38**

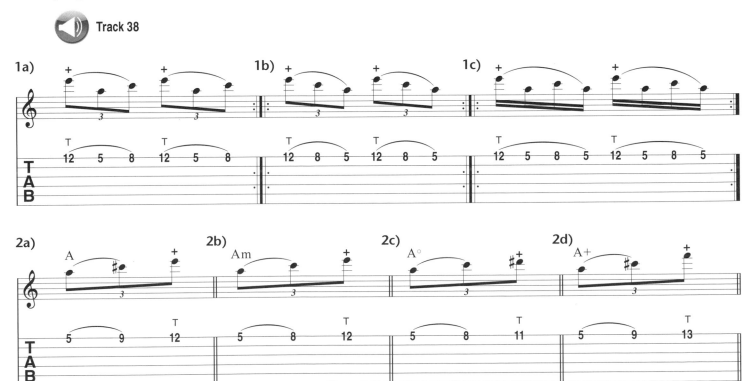

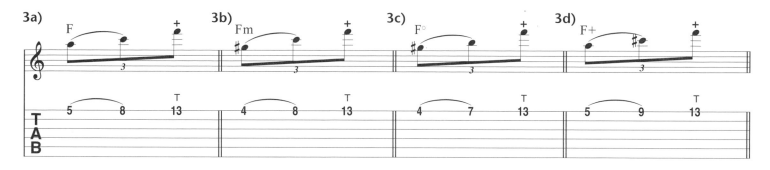

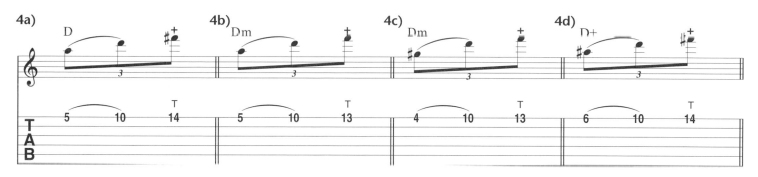

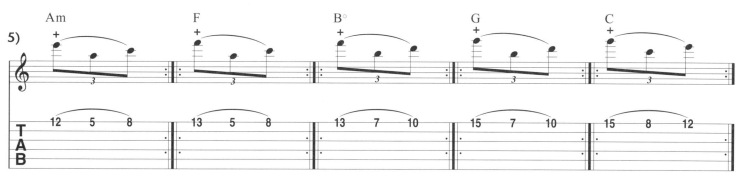

Pentatonic Tapping Licks

Tapping can also be applied to pentatonic shapes. Here we see some A minor pentatonic tapping licks.

🔊 Track 39

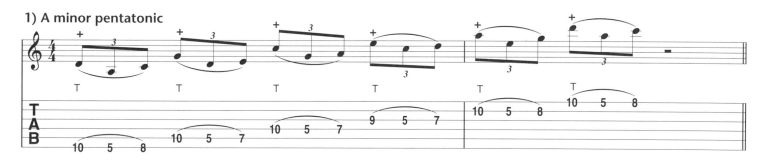

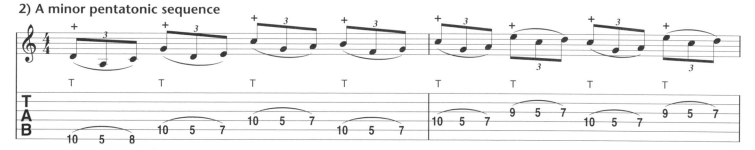

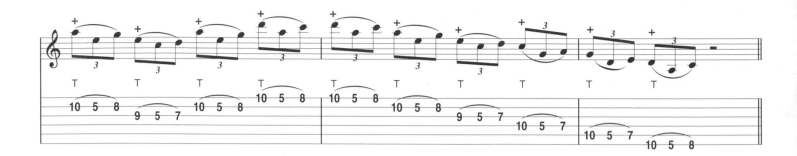

Open-String Tapping Licks

Open strings are sometimes included in tapping licks as well. This can lend an even greater angular sound to your lines.

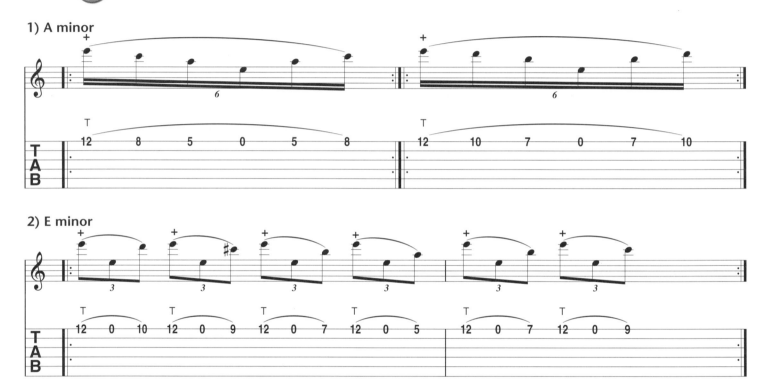

Track 40

1) A minor

2) E minor

Pedal-Tone Tapping Licks

The pedal-tone technique we learned earlier sounds great when used with tapping. Here we see a lick in A minor.

Track 41

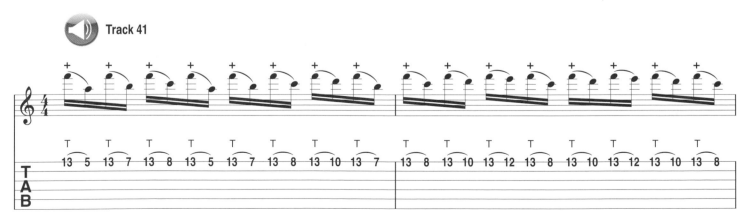

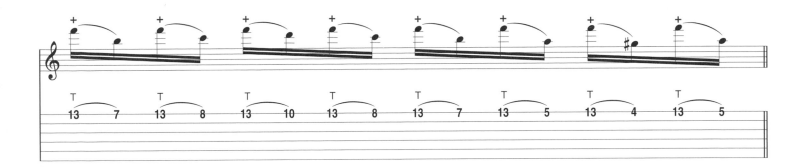

Tapped Slides

Sometimes, players will tap on a note and then slide that right-hand finger while holding the tapped note. This is a bit more difficult and requires a bit of practice. Here are some examples of licks that involve tapped slides.

Track 42

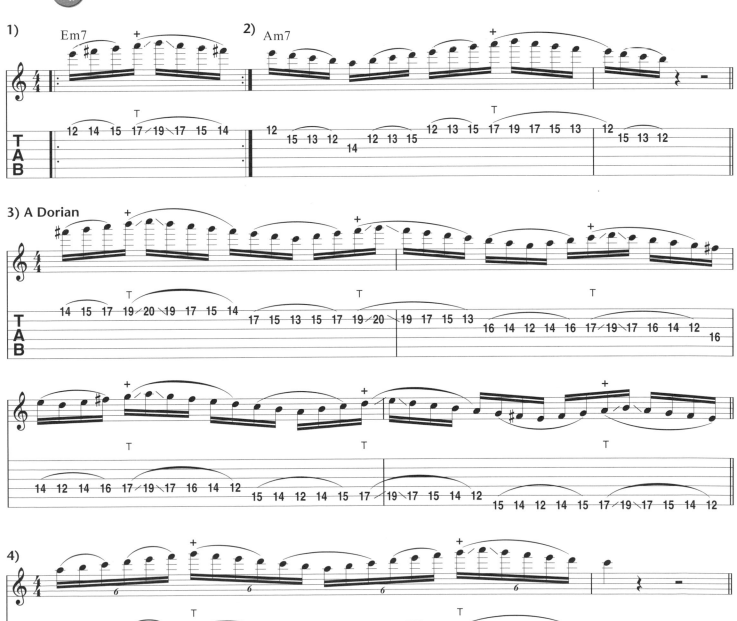

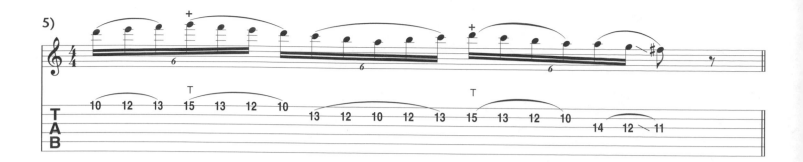

Scalar Tapping Licks

Here we see tapping applied to a four-note-per-string scalar pattern. This can be applied to any scale shape, so be sure to try it over some other scales. When ascending, you can start off with a pull-off from your right hand. The first note of each following beat (on the new string) should begin with a right-hand finger plucking the string.

Track 43

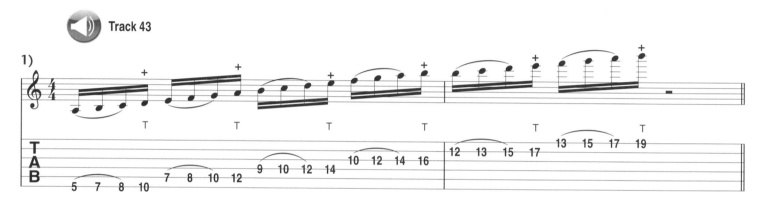

Descending is a bit easier. You simply begin each new string with a tap and pull off to the remaining notes.

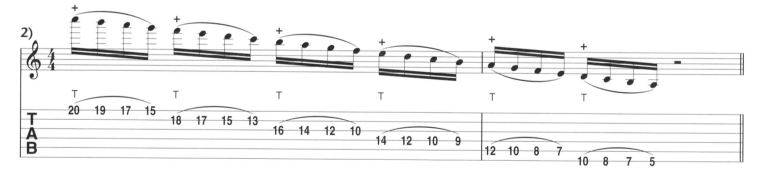

These two examples apply the scalar tapping approach to one string.

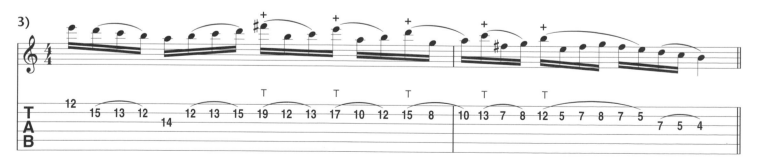

4)

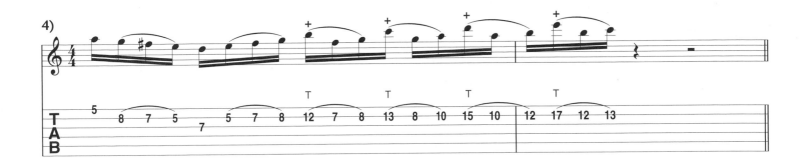

Eight-Fingered Tapping

As if tapped slides weren't hard enough, along comes *eight-fingered tapping!* This requires a little practice. The following example demonstrates this technique.

🔊 **Track 44**

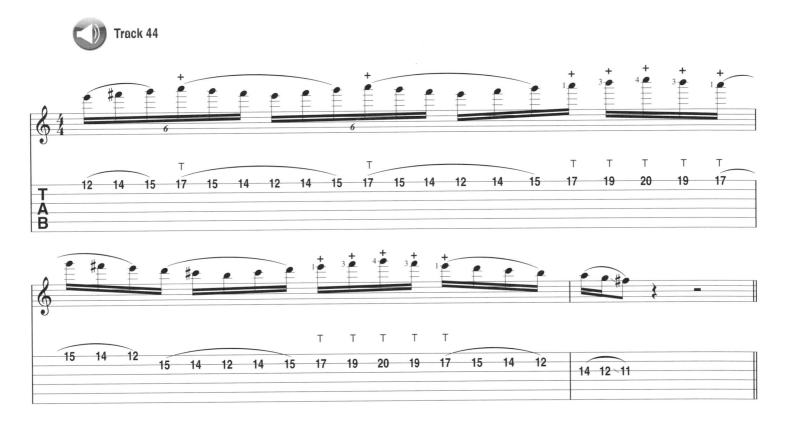

LESSON 3

HARMONY AND THEORY

Substitutions

If we look at a 7th chord with all its extensions, we can see that other 7th chords exist within it. Let's take a look at Cmaj13. Here we see all the notes present in the chord:

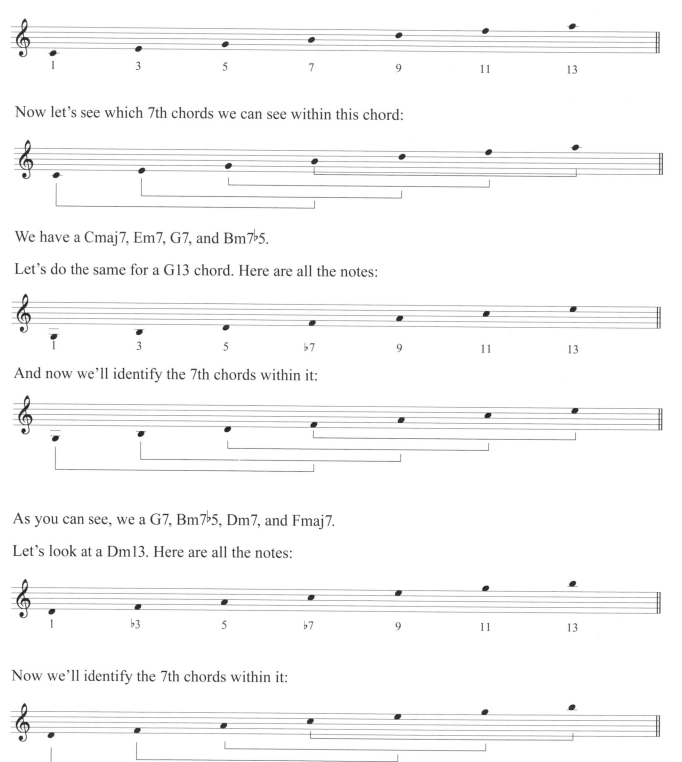

Now let's see which 7th chords we can see within this chord:

We have a Cmaj7, Em7, G7, and Bm7♭5.

Let's do the same for a G13 chord. Here are all the notes:

And now we'll identify the 7th chords within it:

As you can see, we a G7, Bm7♭5, Dm7, and Fmaj7.

Let's look at a Dm13. Here are all the notes:

Now we'll identify the 7th chords within it:

We have Dm7, Fmaj7, Am7, and Cmaj7.

Let's look at substitutions for Fmaj13♯11. Here are all the notes:

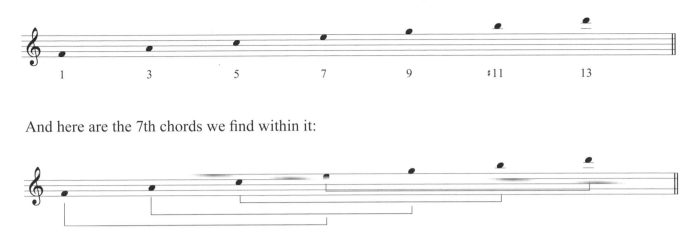

1   3   5   7   9   ♯11   13

And here are the 7th chords we find within it:

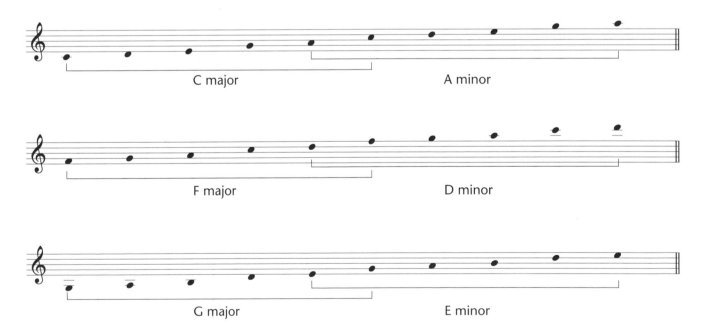

Fmaj7, Am7, Cmaj7, and Em7.

Pentatonic Substitutions

When we harmonized the major scale, we found out that there are major triads on the 1st, 4th, and 5th degrees and minor triads on the 2nd, 3rd, and 6th degrees. The major and minor triads are all related by a minor 3rd. We also know that in the major scale are two pentatonic scales: I (C major) pentatonic and vi (A minor) pentatonic. They are a minor 3rd apart.

You can find this same relationship within the other major and minor triads of the scale:

      IV (F major) pentatonic and ii (D minor) pentatonic

      V (G major) pentatonic and iii (E minor) pentatonic

This is demonstrated below:

C major   A minor

F major   D minor

G major   E minor

As you can see, all three major and minor pentatonics are in the major scale. That means you can use all three minor /major pentatonics for all the modes of the major scale. Here are some examples:

D Dorian: You can use D minor (i), E minor (ii), and A minor (v)

E Phrygian: You can use E minor (i), D minor (vii), and A minor (iv)

A Aeolian: You can use A minor (i), D minor (iv), and E minor (v)

C Ionian: You can use C major (I), F major (IV), and G major (V)

F Lydian: You can use F major (I), G (II), and C major (V)

G Mixolydian: You can use G major (I), F (VII), and C major (IV)

RHYTHM CONCEPTS

Groups of Four in 3/4

Occasionally, you will see 4 tuplets in a 3/4 environment. This means you have four quarter notes in the time of three quarter notes ("4 over 3"). This may seem impossible to count, but when you subdivide the three quarter notes into sixteenth notes, it becomes fairly easy. Simply tie three sixteenths together, and you've got it. See below for an example:

Practice this new rhythm with other rhythm figures in 3/4. Make up your own exercises and try to use this rhythm for your writing and playing. Here are some more examples of different rhythms in 3/4:

Rhythm Exercise 29

1) 7 attacks per measure

2) 6 attacks per measure

3) 5 attacks per measure

Rhythm Exercise 30

1) 4 attacks per measure

2) 3 attacks per measure

Major ii–V–I Progressions

Here we see several different voicings for the ii–V–I progression:

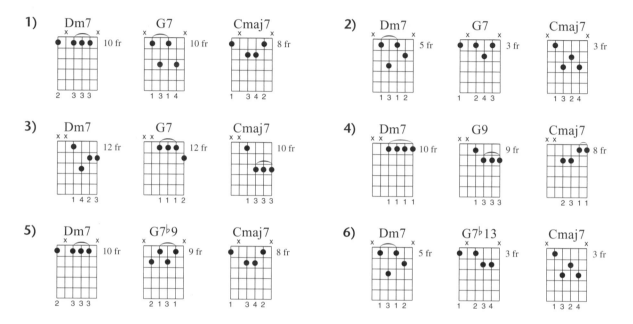

Minor ii–V–i Progressions

And here we find voicings for the minor version:

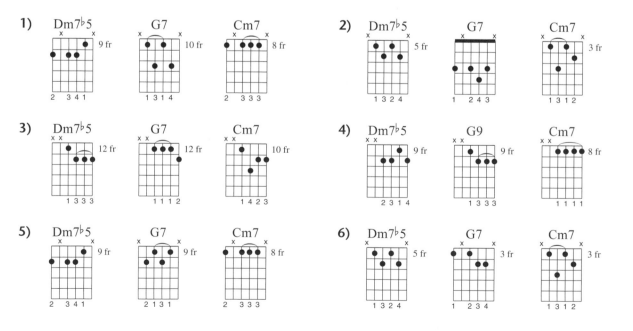

SIGHT-READING

Chord Chart Reading Exercise 5

Chord Chart Reading Exercise 6

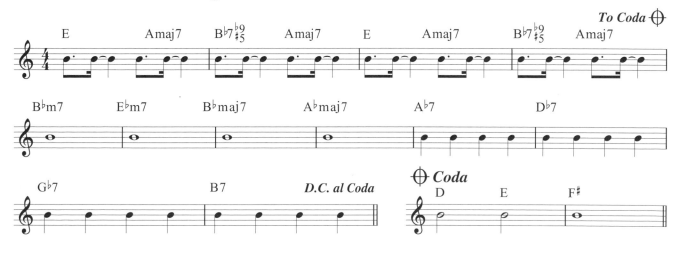

SCALES AND TECHNIQUES: SWEEP PICKING

We talked briefly about economy picking earlier as an alternative to alternate picking. *Sweep picking* takes economy picking a bit further. The reason it is called economy picking is because it is more efficient (economic) than alternate picking. Generally, economy picking is used to describe this technique when used in scalar playing, while sweep picking is used to describe the technique when applied to arpeggios. Let's look at an example in A minor:

Alternate picking: you need a total of 18 strokes

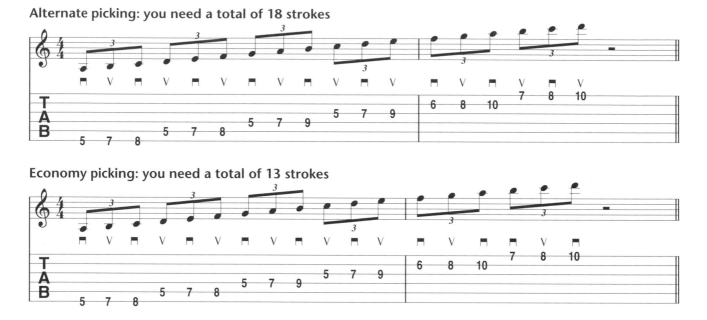

Economy picking: you need a total of 13 strokes

The concept is that you use the same direction of your pick whenever possible. If you move from bass to treble strings (sixth to first string), you use downstrokes to change strings. If you move from treble to bass strings (first to sixth string), you use upstrokes to change strings. This means you need an odd number of notes on each string if you keep the same direction and you need an even number of notes on a string if you want to change direction. Sometimes it will be difficult to keep your line diatonic or to use the same sequence for the whole line. Don't be afraid to use chromatics to fill up your line or skip a note to change the strings. In this way, you can play some sudden intervals which would be hard to play with alternate picking.

Scales

Here we see several examples of this technique applied to scales:

 Track 45

1) A major

178

2) A major

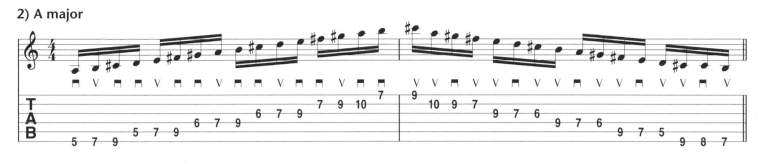

3) A minor

4) A minor

etc.

Triads

This technique can make three-note triads fairly easy to play:

 Track 46

1) Major triads

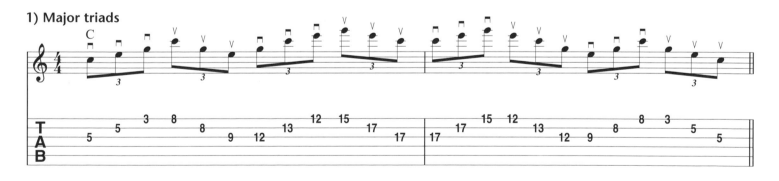

Track 47

2) Minor triads

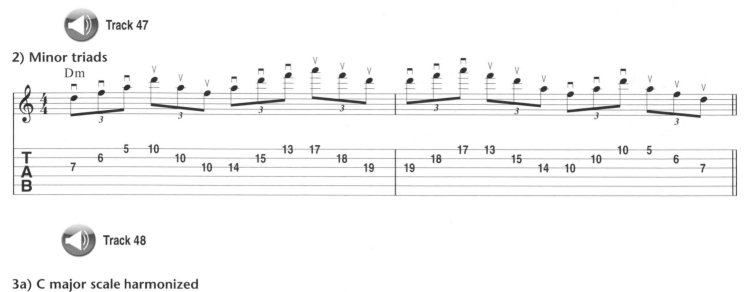

Track 48

3a) C major scale harmonized

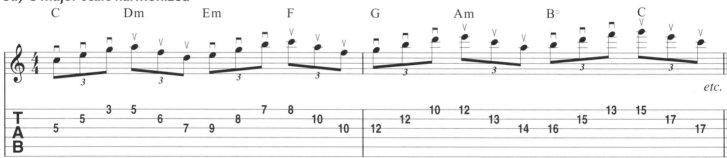

etc.

3b)

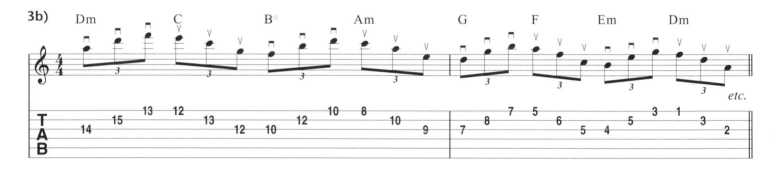

etc.

3c)

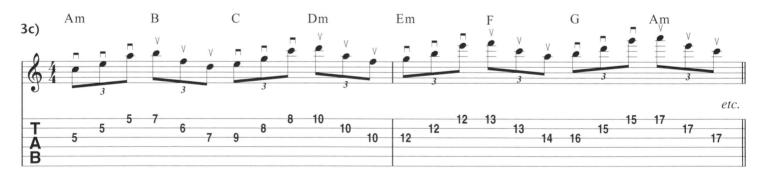

etc.

Track 48

4a)   **4b)**   **4c)**

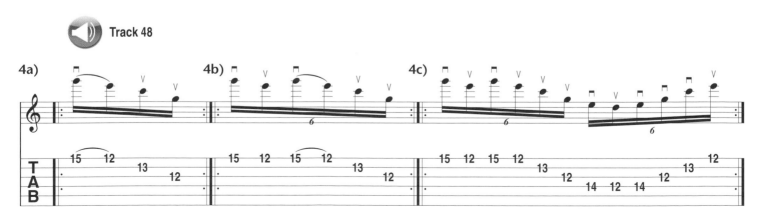

Arpeggios

The most common application of sweep picking lies in full arpeggios. Make sure you're not allowing the notes to ring together. You want it sound like melody, not a chord. Here we see several examples:

Track 50

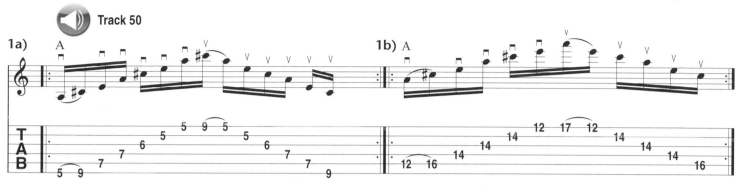

Track 51

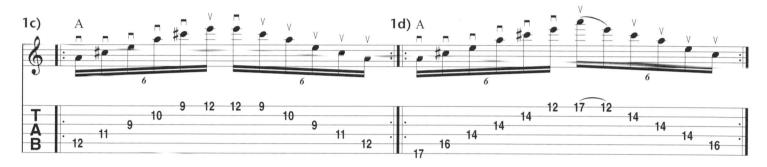

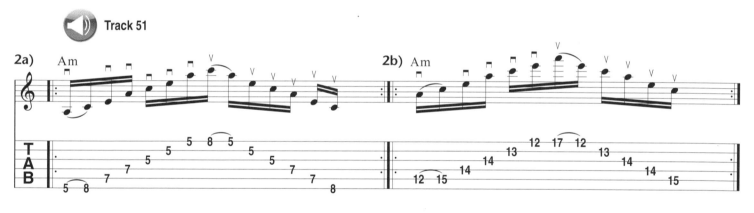

Track 52

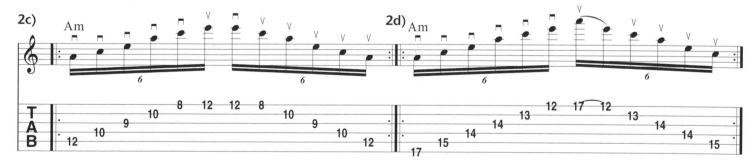

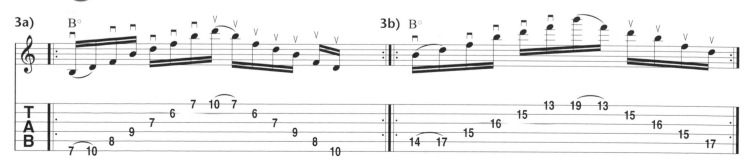

3c)

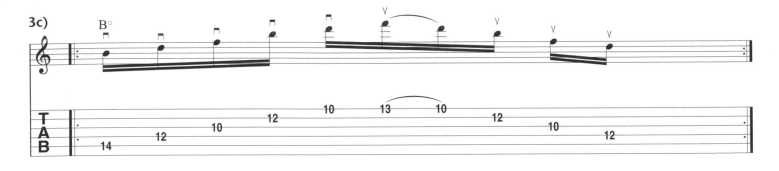

 Track 53

4a) **4b)**

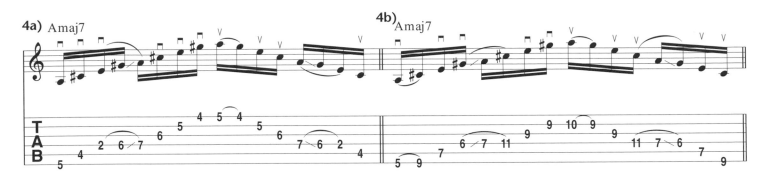

4c) **4d)**

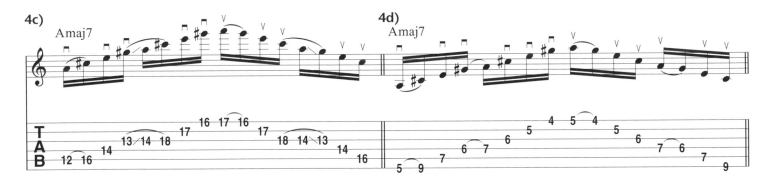

 Track 54

5a) **5b)**

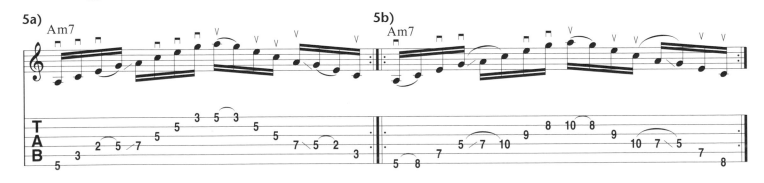

5c) **5d)**

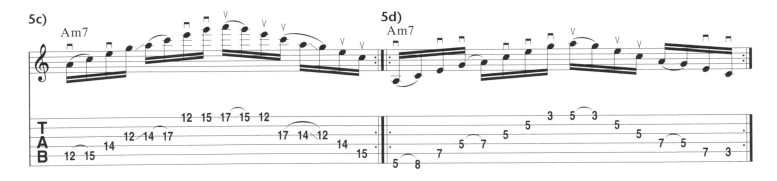

Track 55

6a)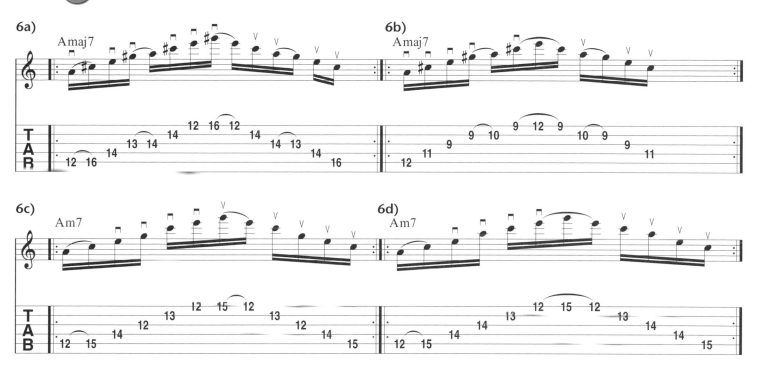

6b)

6c)

6d)

Here we see the C major scale harmonized with 7th chords:

Track 56

7)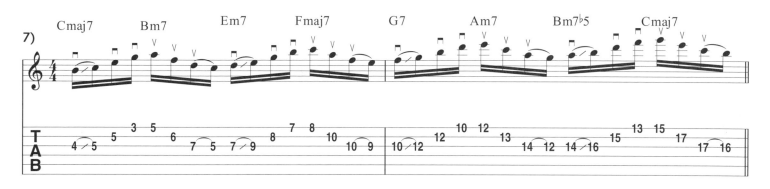

Sweep Picking with Tapping

Sometimes tapping is used in conjunction with sweeping for increased range. This example demonstrates this:

Track 57

8a)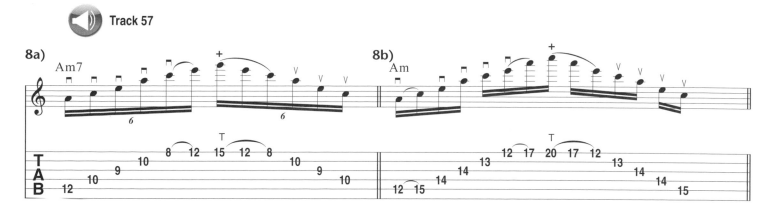

8b)

LESSON 4 • JAZZ

COMMON CHORD PROGRESSIONS

ii–V–I Progressions

1) ii–V–I: major

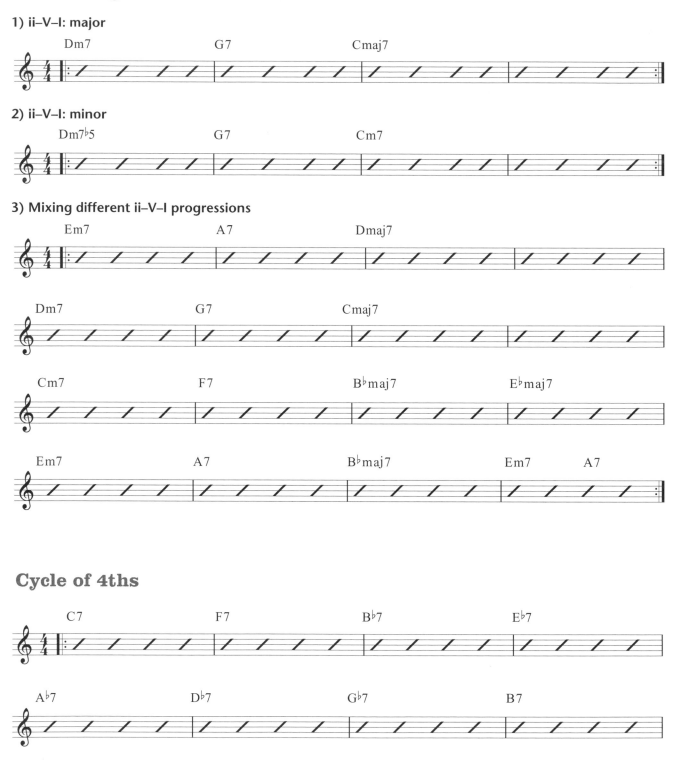

2) ii–V–I: minor

3) Mixing different ii–V–I progressions

Cycle of 4ths

Rhythm Changes

This progression comes from the Gershwin tune "I Got Rhythm." The chord changes have become standard in the jazz repertoire.

Modal Improvisation

These types of changes were popularized by Miles Davis. They consist of long sections on one chord.

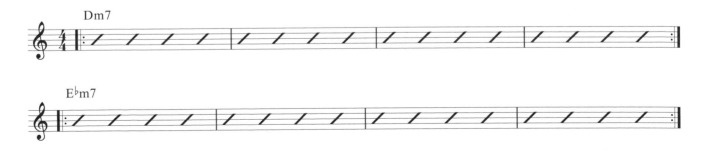

Typical Jazz Standard

These changes have been the basis for many jazz standards:

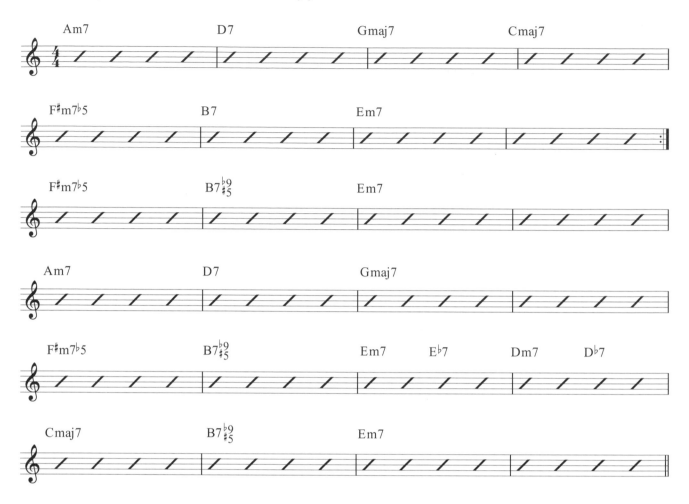

COMMON JAZZ RHYTHMS

Here we see some common chordal rhythms you're likely to see in jazz. Remember that the eighth notes are almost always "swung" (played with a shuffle feel) in jazz. Some ballads are not, but generally most mid-tempo and up-tempo tunes are.

ii–V–I: Ballad

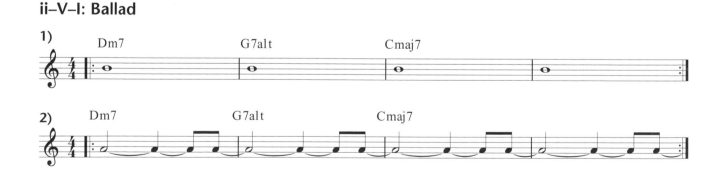

ii–V–I: Medium Swing

IMPROVISING CONCEPTS

Modes

In a standard ii–V–I progression, one obvious choice would be the use of the corresponding mode for each chord. This means that we use Dorian for the ii chord, Mixolydian for the V chord, and Ionian for the I chord. It sounds more natural to our ears if we stay in the same key as long as possible. Below, we see these modes played in the same position in the key of C major:

Dorian

Mixolydian

Ionian

Arpeggios

Another approach is to use the arpeggios for each chord. Below we see an example of this idea:

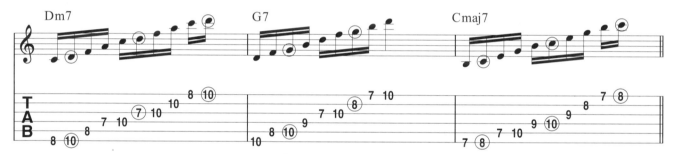

Altered Scale

When the V chord is altered in a progression, it's common to use the *altered* scale. The degrees of this scale are 1–♭2–♭3–3–♯4–♯5–♭7. In G7, this would be (G–A♭–B♭–B–C♯–D♯–F). Here we see an example of this scale in C major:

Dorian

Altered

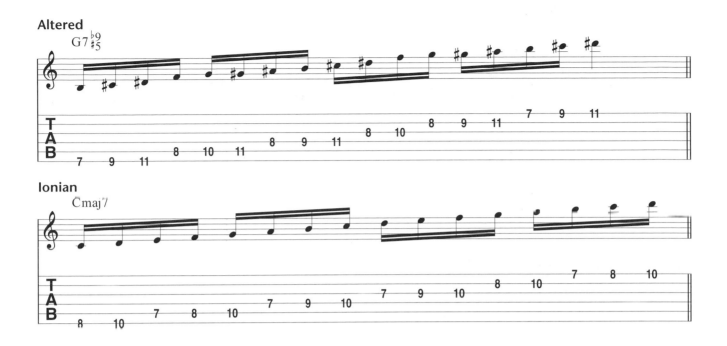

Ionian

The modal and arpeggio approach can also be applied to the minor ii–V–i. Here we see the modes in a ii–V–i in C minor:

Locrian

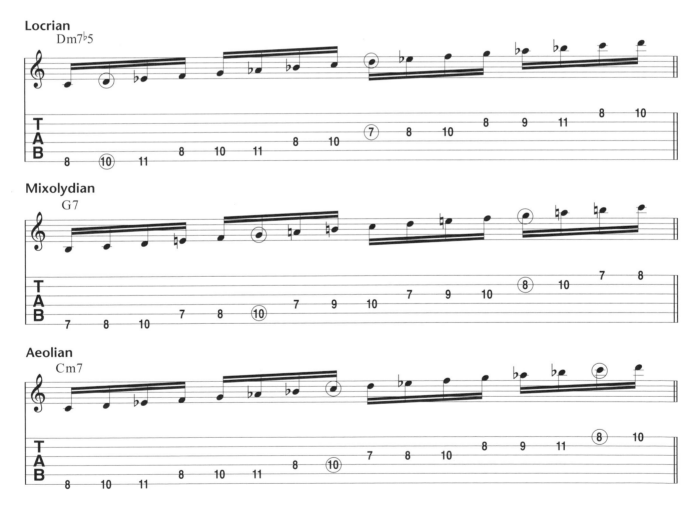

Mixolydian

Aeolian

And now we see the arpeggio approach:

Harmonic Minor Scale

When playing a ii–V–i in a minor key, it is common to use the *harmonic minor scale* over the V chord. This would be the harmonic minor built off the tonic (i) chord, not the V chord. A harmonic minor scale is basically a minor scale with a natural 7 (1–2–♭3–4–5–♭6–7). In C minor, this would be: C–D–E♭–F–G–A♭–B. Below we see the C harmonic minor scale over the G7 chord:

GUITAR NOTATION LEGEND

Guitar Music can be notated three different ways: on a musical staff, in tablature, and in rhythm slashes.

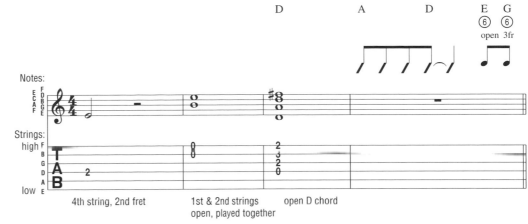

RHYTHM SLASHES are written above the staff. Strum chords in the rhythm indicated. Use the chord diagrams found at the top of the first page of the transcription for the appropriate chord voicings. Round noteheads indicate single notes.

THE MUSICAL STAFF shows pitches and rhythms and is divided by bar lines into measures. Pitches are named after the first seven letters of the alphabet.

TABLATURE graphically represents the guitar fingerboard. Each horizontal line represents a a string, and each number represents a fret.

4th string, 2nd fret

1st & 2nd strings open, played together

open D chord

Definitions for Special Guitar Notation

HALF-STEP BEND: Strike the note and bend up 1/2 step.

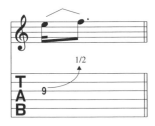

WHOLE-STEP BEND: Strike the note and bend up one step.

GRACE NOTE BEND: Strike the note and immediately bend up as indicated.

SLIGHT (MICROTONE) BEND: Strike the note and bend up 1/4 step.

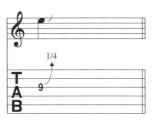

BEND AND RELEASE: Strike the note and bend up as indicated, then release back to the original note. Only the first note is struck.

PRE-BEND: Bend the note as indicated, then strike it.

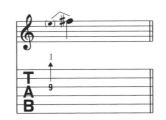

PRE-BEND AND RELEASE: Bend the note as indicated. Strike it and release the bend back to the original note.

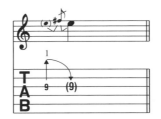

UNISON BEND: Strike the two notes simultaneously and bend the lower note up to the pitch of the higher.

VIBRATO: The string is vibrated by rapidly bending and releasing the note with the fretting hand.

WIDE VIBRATO: The pitch is varied to a greater degree by vibrating with the fretting hand.

HAMMER-ON: Strike the first (lower) note with one finger, then sound the higher note (on the same string) with another finger by fretting it without picking.

PULL-OFF: Place both fingers on the notes to be sounded. Strike the first note and without picking, pull the finger off to sound the second (lower) note.

LEGATO SLIDE: Strike the first note and then slide the same fret-hand finger up or down to the second note. The second note is not struck.

SHIFT SLIDE: Same as legato slide, except the second note is struck.

TRILL: Very rapidly alternate between the notes indicated by continuously hammering on and pulling off.

TAPPING: Hammer ("tap") the fret indicated with the pick-hand index or middle finger and pull off to the note fretted by the fret hand.

NATURAL HARMONIC: Strike the note while the fret-hand lightly touches the string directly over the fret indicated.

PINCH HARMONIC: The note is fretted normally and a harmonic is produced by adding the edge of the thumb or the tip of the index finger of the pick hand to the normal pick attack.

HARP HARMONIC: The note is fretted normally and a harmonic is produced by gently resting the pick hand's index finger directly above the indicated fret (in parentheses) while the pick hand's thumb or pick assists by plucking the appropriate string.

PICK SCRAPE: The edge of the pick is rubbed down (or up) the string, producing a scratchy sound.

MUFFLED STRINGS: A percussive sound is produced by laying the fret hand across the string(s) without depressing, and striking them with the pick hand.

PALM MUTING: The note is partially muted by the pick hand lightly touching the string(s) just before the bridge.

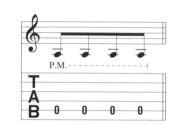

RAKE: Drag the pick across the strings indicated with a single motion.

TREMOLO PICKING: The note is picked as rapidly and continuously as possible.

ARPEGGIATE: Play the notes of the chord indicated by quickly rolling them from bottom to top.

VIBRATO BAR DIVE AND RETURN: The pitch of the note or chord is dropped a specified number of steps (in rhythm) then returned to the original pitch.

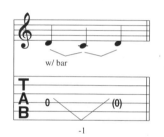

VIBRATO BAR SCOOP: Depress the bar just before striking the note, then quickly release the bar.

VIBRATO BAR DIP: Strike the note and then immediately drop a specified number of steps, then release back to the original pitch.

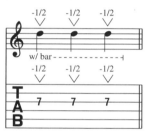

Additional Musical Definitions

(accent)	• Accentuate note (play it louder)	
(accent)	• Accentuate note with great intensity	
(staccato)	• Play the note short	
	• Downstroke	
	• Upstroke	

D.S. al Coda • Go back to the sign (𝄋), then play until the measure marked "*To Coda*," then skip to the section labelled "**Coda**."

D.C. al Fine • Go back to the beginning of the song and play until the measure marked "*Fine*" (end).

Rhy. Fig. • Label used to recall a recurring accompaniment pattern (usually chordal).

Riff • Label used to recall composed, melodic lines (usually single notes) which recur.

Fill • Label used to identify a brief melodic figure which is to be inserted into the arrangement.

Rhy. Fill • A chordal version of a Fill.

tacet • Instrument is silent (drops out).

• Repeat measures between signs.

• When a repeated section has different endings, play the first ending only the first time and the second ending only the second time.

NOTE: Tablature numbers in parentheses mean:
1. The note is being sustained over a system (note in standard notation is tied), or
2. The note is sustained, but a new articulation (such as a hammer-on, pull-off, slide or vibrato begins), or
3. The note is a barely audible "ghost" note (note in standard notation is also in parentheses).